# HARD CORE CARNIVORE

Dedicated to my parents for their incomparable support and encouragement.

★ JESS PRYLES ★

# HARD CORE CARNIVORE

## COOK MEAT LIKE YOU MEAN IT

murdoch books

Sydney | London

# CONTENTS

# INTRODUCTION

My name is Jess Pryles and I am a Hardcore Carnivore.

I used to be intimidated by the idea of cooking meat. I shied away from the meat department at grocery stores because the selection was overwhelming, and I wasn't confident in my own cooking abilities. I didn't understand the differences between the steaks, nor the right way to cook the different cuts of meat.

So, I decided to change all that. I set about educating myself on all things meat-related, particularly beef (which is my personal favourite). I learned how to cook it, where it comes from, which are the best tasting cuts, which are the most economical but flavourful cuts, the difference between grass- and grain-fed meats, understanding various breeds of animal, and so much more.

My initial desire to simply be able to cook a decent steak at home ended up morphing into a full-blown obsession, and it's a journey that has led me from my birthplace of Melbourne, Australia, to my new home of Austin, Texas.

I've visited ranches, farms, slaughterhouses, butcher shops and even 'meat university', gathering knowledge, tips and know-how, fascinated by the science behind the cooking. Put simply, I'm a meat nerd, and now I get to share both my discoveries and recipes with you.

Having spent so much time in Texas (even before becoming a 'Texpat'), the food I create has naturally taken on influences from Tex Mex, Cajun and Southern cooking, which is reflected in my recipes. I hope you enjoy re-creating them in your own homes, and that you're inspired to pick up at least one cut of meat you haven't tried before.

## HOW TO USE THIS BOOK

* All bacon used in my recipes is American-style belly bacon (without the loin part that is found in Australian short-cut bacon). Streaky bacon is an equivalent for this.

* Though temperatures in the book are given in both Celsius and Fahrenheit, I prefer to cook using Fahrenheit, particularly for internal meat temperatures. As it has a broader scale than Celsius, Fahrenheit offers more precise measurements, which are particularly important when referring to degrees of doneness.

* I use coarse Morton kosher salt for all my recipes (some salts are 'saltier' than others, as explained further on pages 18–20). If you can't find kosher salt, I recommend sea salt flakes (which you can easily crush with your fingers) as an alternative.

* When you see the term 'grilling' in this book, it refers to direct heat cooking over coals or propane/gas. 'Barbecue' refers to low and slow cooking with indirect heat.

* I prefer to use cast-iron skillets and heavy-based enamelled cast-iron pots for most of my stovetop cooking, unless otherwise specified.

Here's to good cooking and great meals.

*Jess.*

# FORE QUARTER: THE INFORMATION

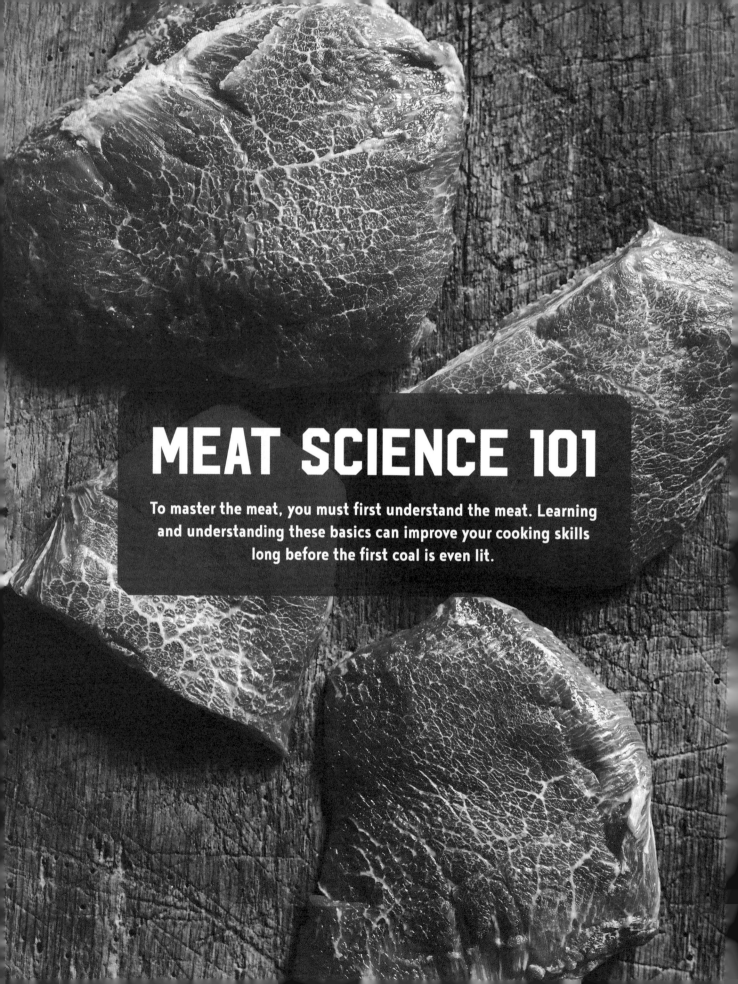

# MEAT SCIENCE 101

To master the meat, you must first understand the meat. Learning and understanding these basics can improve your cooking skills long before the first coal is even lit.

## RESTING MEAT

Nearly every whole muscle recipe in this book has an instruction to rest the meat after cooking. Have you ever cut into a steak right after cooking and watched those precious juices flood out onto your board? Well, that spillage is the exact reason you should always rest meat before cutting.

Muscles are made up of tightly bundled protein strands that wring even tighter together when heat is applied, pushing water to their edges during cooking. Resting allows these fibres to relax, and enables that moisture to return down the strands and redistribute evenly. The resting time is proportionate to the cooking time, so a quickly seared steak may only need a 10-minute rest, while a long, slow roast may need 30 minutes or more.

## CUTTING AGAINST THE GRAIN

You've heard the adage to always slice meat against the grain, but how do you find the grain and why do we do this? Each muscle has fibres that run alongside one another in a single direction, and this is the grain. The grain is more clearly visible on certain cuts like the flank, skirt and tri-tip. Confusingly, large cuts that are comprised of several muscles might have several directions of grain, like brisket, where the grain switches halfway through the cut.

Finding the grain and cutting against it means slicing perpendicular to the direction that the fibres are running. Doing this lessens the resistance of each bite, and makes a dramatic difference to the eating quality and tenderness of the cut.

## AGEING BEEF

Ageing is the process of holding meat (primarily beef, which benefits most from the process) for an extended period from the slaughter date to the consumption date. As unpleasant as it sounds, the process of ageing meat is essentially carefully controlled decomposition, and is used to promote tenderness and, in some cases, improve taste. Ageing needs to occur for at least 12–14 days to yield any discernible results.

Wet ageing simply refers to product that is vacuum-packed, and therefore 'wet' from sitting in its own liquids. It's a faster and cheaper process than dry ageing, and more cost effective because there is no loss of mass due to shrinkage. The downside to wet ageing is the shorter window before the quality of the meat starts deteriorating, which is exacerbated by the constant opening and closing of domestic refrigerators. When wet aged for too long, the meat will start to take on an unpleasant taste that can be described as sour, minerally and serumy. It's also at the mercy of the supply chain, since exposure to unstable temperatures (such as moving from freezer to different fridges) creates more 'weep' (liquid) in the bag, which can cause an unappealing spongy texture from unwanted microbial growth.

Dry ageing works by exposing large subprimal cuts (see Meat-speak, page 12) to a carefully controlled environment with precise temperature and humidity levels. At the same time that tenderness is being increased, the flavour of the beef is being intensified by a combination of bacteria, enzyme breakdown and oxidation. It's a far more expensive process thanks to the equipment required, plus the yield of the final saleable product is sacrificed to shrinkage and trimming. When dry ageing pushes beyond a 60-day mark or thereabouts, it starts morphing into a kind of delicacy, not unlike stinky cheese. The more it ages, the funkier it gets.

The most important distinction between the two different methods is that dry ageing influences taste and tenderness, whereas wet ageing affects only tenderness. My personal preference is for dry-aged product, aged between 40 and 60 days.

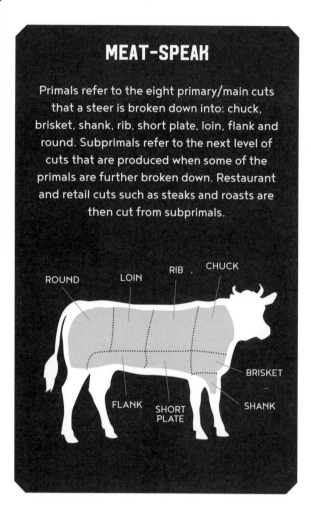

## MARBLING

Marbling is the industry term for the delicate lines of fat that appear within meat. It refers specifically to intramuscular fat, which forms within the muscle itself. The fat that forms between muscles (such as the outside of a rib-eye steak) is known as intermuscular, also called seam fat.

Marbling is hugely important to the eating quality of meat, because it influences the degree of both flavour and tenderness. In fact, most international meat-grading systems have the degree of marbling as the primary factor in grade influence, along with a few other variables. Simply, fat is flavour.

Generally, marbling only comes into play when talking about beef or some of the heritage breeds of pork. Wagyu beef is so highly prized because of its incredible genetic predisposition to intense marbling. Meats like venison or chicken have a very low to negligible degree of marbling.

## MAILLARD REACTION

It's the standard we are all trying to achieve on our steaks, roasts and even hamburger patties— a delicious browned exterior crust. The browning of meat is a process called the Maillard reaction, and a successful sear not only improves colour and outside texture, but intensifies flavour and creates appealing aromas.

The Maillard reaction is a chemical reaction between amino acids and sugars, and is in fact a different process from straight browning. Sometimes it can be challenging to achieve this crust, and there's one simple factor that makes all the difference: moisture. Maillard occurs with dry conditions and high heat, so eliminating as much moisture as possible before you begin cooking puts you ahead of the curve. At the very least, I always pat my meat down thoroughly with paper towel before searing it, to ensure the surface is as dry as possible.

Achieving a desirable crust takes a combination of a dry exterior to start, plus patience in the pan.

# THE IMPORTANCE OF TEMPERATURE

No matter which protein you choose, or which cut you select, or the method you opt to cook it, the variable of temperature is the most significant influencing factor to your success when cooking meat.

## THERMOMETERS

A meat thermometer is the most important thing you can invest in to become a meat-maestro in your own kitchen. And not just any meat thermometer, but a good one. Those little sticks with the dial faces that you can pick up for less than the cost of a steak are really not going to cut it—too often they aren't properly calibrated, offer unreliable readings or take too long to yield a result. Put it this way, the small amount you'll invest once in a quality instant-read thermometer is totally worth it compared to the cost of overcooked meat.

## ACCURACY

There are so many variables when it comes to meat cookery. How thick is the cut? Are you cooking grain- or grass-fed product? Which cooking method are you using? What kind of heat source are you using? Despite the myriad of influencing factors, cooking to temperature is always consistent and reliable. This is also related to food safety, as certain proteins such as chicken and pork need to reach a minimum internal temperature to kill off bacteria and be considered safe to eat.

## TEMPERATURE AND THE ART OF DEEP-FRYING

If you've ever wanted to become an expert in all things golden brown, you're going to need temperature on your side. The precise heat of the oil is imperative to achieving a successful crispy crunch, and makes all the difference between a soggy and sublime result. Use your thermometer to check the temperature of the oil between batches, to make sure it has come back up to optimum temp.

## GRILL TEMPERATURES

Throughout the book, you'll find references to the temperature of your grill or smoker. Again, 'grill' refers to a direct heat coal or gas unit, whereas barbecue/smoker refers to a pit or indirect cooker. If your grill doesn't have a temperature gauge, you can fairly reliably use the hand method, which measures how many seconds you can hold your hand over the heat before you need to pull it away. Obviously, this is not a test of fortitude, so be sure to move your hand before you burn yourself!

Temperatures for the grill are as follows:

**HIGH:** 230–315°C (450–600°F): 1–3 seconds
**MEDIUM-HIGH:** 200–230°C (400–450°F): 4–5 seconds
**MEDIUM:** 180–200°C (350–400°F): 6–7 seconds
**MEDIUM-LOW:** 150–180°C (300–350°F): 8–10 seconds
**LOW:** 120–150°C (250–300°F): 10–12 seconds

## CELSIUS OR FAHRENHEIT?

Traditionally, the use of either Celsius or Fahrenheit was determined by international borders, but this is changing. The barbecue community in Australia commonly uses Fahrenheit as the preferred unit of measurement. This is due both to the in-built gauges on the smokers being displayed in Fahrenheit, and also because most reference material and recipes are from the USA and therefore are written in Fahrenheit. More significantly, Fahrenheit offers a broader range of scale, and therefore more precision, than Celsius does. For your convenience, references to temperatures in this book are given in both Celsius and Fahrenheit, and all the Celsius temperatures have been rounded up or down to make them as accurate as possible. Personally, I prefer to work exclusively in Fahrenheit.

Nearly all thermometers (even the cheap ones) will either display both Celsius and Fahrenheit, or allow you to toggle between them.

## DONENESS

'Doneness' is the degree to which meat is cooked. You find it most frequently mentioned in conjunction with steaks; for example: rare, medium or (perish the thought) well done.

The Doneness Chart pertains only to whole-muscle red meat, since proteins such as chicken and pork need to be cooked to a minimum temperature to be considered safe for consumption.

Doneness is also the reason you need the aforementioned meat thermometer because it's determined by temperature (and not by squeezing the heel of your palm!).

Temperature is also referenced a great deal in low and slow cooking, both as the temperature to cook at and also as an important indicator for the minimum degree the meat needs to reach to be ready. For example, it's commonly accepted that pork shoulder (also called butt) needs to reach at least 88°C (190°F) before it will 'give' and become tender.

And while on the subject of doneness, I would be remiss not to address the controversial 'rare' burger. Any meat scientist would be completely grossed out by the idea of a patty that's pink in the middle (and even more horrified by the idea of carpaccio or tartare). And here's why: when you sear a steak you are killing off any bacteria on the outside but the inner muscle remains sterile, having never been previously exposed (which is why we can eat rare steaks). But when you make minced (ground) beef, you're taking the bacteria-laden meat to make a hot mess of microbial activity. So, technically speaking, no, pink burgers and steak tartare are not by-the-book food safe, and if you want to be absolutely sure you're being safe, cook your ground beef to at least 71°C (160°F). BUT, if you are using very fresh meat from a reputable source, you mitigate the chances of anything going wrong (case in point: the many kilograms of raw steak I have consumed over the years without any misfortune).

### TEMPERATURE TIP
Remember that meat will climb at least a few degrees in temperature after it is removed from the heat source and rested, and you should take that into account when you pick the optimal temperature to cease the cooking process.

### DONENESS CHART

| RARE | 52–54°C (125–130°F) |
|---|---|
| MEDIUM–RARE | 54–57°C (130–135°F) |
| MEDIUM | 57–63°C (135–145°F) |
| MEDIUM–WELL | 63–68°C (145–155°F) |
| WELL DONE | 68°C+ (155°F+) |

### SAFE TEMPERATURES

| GROUND MEAT | 71°C (160°F) |
|---|---|
| PORK | 63°C (145°F) |
| CHICKEN | 74°C (165°F) |

An instant-read
thermometer is a vital tool
for a meat cook.

# THE ALCHEMY OF SALT

If temperature has the most significant influence on meat, without doubt salt is a close runner up. Adequately seasoning meat makes all the difference between a bland result and a flavoursome one. Let's take a look at some of the science behind salt.

## THE RELATIONSHIP BETWEEN SALT AND MEAT

The humble white grain that we sprinkle so liberally on our food is actually an antimicrobial chemical compound known as sodium chloride.

When salt hits the surface of any meat, the process of osmosis begins immediately—moisture is drawn out of the meat towards the crystals. This creates a slick watery surface that eventually dissolves the salt crystals. If left long enough, the process of diffusion then draws this salty brine back into the meat.

Salt also acts as a tenderiser. If you think of proteins as little bundles of tightly packed strings, the salt acts to destroy the characteristic properties of the proteins, effectively loosening the strings from one another, creating a more tender bite—a process known as denaturing.

## TIMING YOUR SEASONING

This process of osmosis and denaturing takes time, so timing your seasoning correctly is hugely important. You have two options when it comes to timing your seasoning:

* Salt the meat immediately before cooking, before the salt has a chance to draw the moisture to the surface and delay the onset of the Maillard reaction (page 12).

OR

* Apply seasoning and leave the meat at least 40-45 minutes, so any moisture that is drawn to the surface has the opportunity to reabsorb.

Essentially, try to steer clear of salting your meat anywhere during the 10-30 minute mark prior to cooking. All you'll be doing is drawing moisture out without giving it the opportunity to soak back in.

## DEEP SEASONING

Also known as dry brining, deep seasoning is a method used primarily with steaks, taking the concept of salting in advance and extending it well beyond a few hours. To deep season, sprinkle your steak generously with salt then place it (uncovered) on a rack above a drip tray in the fridge for up to 3 days. The idea is to allow enough time for the salty brine to reabsorb and penetrate the meat completely, but also to have a pronounced drying effect on the surface, which promotes an incredible crust when cooking.

Deep seasoning has an impressive effect on both taste and tenderness, but if you do try this method, there are a few things you need to know:

* For discernible results, leave the steak to deep season for at least 24 and up to 72 hours.
* Make sure you are using steak at least 2.5 cm (1 inch) thick.
* Do not rinse or apply more salt to the steak before cooking it.
* Use meat of absolute freshness.
* Consider leaving an open box of bicarbonate of soda (baking soda) in the fridge to absorb any odours that may taint the meat.

## THERE IS NO SUCH THING AS A STANDARD TEASPOON OF SALT

Throughout the book, you will see the instruction 'salt to taste'. While that can be frustrating for those who feel the need or want to follow a recipe precisely, it's done with good reason: some salts are in fact saltier than others, and it's rare for any two types or brands of salt to have the same degree of potency.

Despite all salt being the same compound, variation occurs because of the density; that is, how much space, or air, is in each crystal. This dictates how much sodium chloride actually comprises that crystal. To simplify, some types of salt have a greater amount of salt per crystal, so they taste saltier.

The only way to combat this is to measure salt by weight, not volume, but that's not very practical in a domestic setting. So instead, you are encouraged to salt to taste—and since you should be tasting your food and will likely have an individual preference for how salty you like things to taste, that should work out well.

I cook using only coarse Morton kosher salt. Kosher salt is a type of salt that is used in the process of koshering meat. Chefs and barbecue folk prefer it because the larger grains are easier to pinch and distribute evenly, plus since it's about half as salty as table salt you are less likely to over-salt while still being liberal with your sprinkle. Outside of the USA, Kosher salt is available in some delis and specialty food stores, but if you can't find it I recommend sea salt flakes (which you can easily crush with your fingers) as an alternative.

Most importantly, be aware that different brands and types of salt have differing levels of saltiness and varying weights. So, if you use something other than kosher salt, you may want to adjust the measurements according to what you are using.

## TYPES OF SALTS

| SALT TYPE | WEIGHT (per tablespoon) |
| --- | --- |
| Iodised table salt | 22.2 grams |
| Sea salt crystals | 18.6 grams |
| Sea salt flakes | 9.1 grams |
| Pink rock salt | 21.1 grams |
| Fleur de sel | 15.7 grams |
| Kosher salt | 18.9 grams |

# CONFIGURING A GRILL FOR TWO-ZONE COOKING

The two-zone set up configures a grill to facilitate indirect cooking, which is far more gentle than direct heat cooking. Often the hot zone is used to sear the meat at the beginning or end of the cooking process, as with the reverse sear method (page 27). Once set up, the two-zone configuration creates both hotter and cooler zones within the same grill. Though it's most prominently used with charcoal grills, the two-zone set up is possible with gas grills, too.

## FOR A CHARCOAL GRILL

Light a chimney of coals and, once glowing and ashed over, pile them on one side of the grill unit, leaving the other side clear and empty. If you do not require direct heat at all, you may want to arrange the coals along the outside of the grill in a ring formation, particularly if you have a round-shaped grill. This will make the entire central zone indirect.

## FOR A GAS GRILL

Light one of the end burners, leaving the others off. For example, if you have a three-burner grill, light the very left burner, and consider the right hand side the indirect zone.

# THE REVERSE SEAR METHOD

**Without overstating it, the reverse sear method has completely revolutionised the way meat enthusiasts cook their steaks, and with good reason. It is a nearly foolproof method for cooking a medium-rare steak, where the perfect pinkness will stretch edge to edge without any gradient of grey.**

Traditionally, restaurants would sear steak over a very hot surface, then finish the cooking process in the oven until the desired internal temperature was reached. As the name suggests, reverse sear is merely this method in reverse order. Another perk of this technique is that you can eat your steak as soon as the sear is finished, because it has already rested.

Reverse sear refers to any cooking method that starts with a low heat and finishes with a hot sear, and can be executed in a number of ways. The methods following are described for steak, but reverse sear can be applied to any cut of meat that is at least 2.5 cm (1 inch) in thickness. Use it for roasts, loins, backstraps and prime rib.

## OVEN AND PAN

Preheat the oven to 135°C (275°F). Pat the steak dry with paper towel and season well with salt. Lay the steak on a rack positioned over a baking pan, and place in the oven. Cook until the steak reaches your desired internal temperature, which will take around 45–60 minutes. Remove once at temp and rest under foil for 10–15 minutes.

Place a cast-iron or heavy-based pan over high heat, and heat to smoking point. Sear the steak for 1–2 minutes on each side, then serve immediately.

## GRILL

Configure your grill for two-zone cooking. Pat the steak dry with paper towel and season well with salt. Place the steak on the indirect side of the grill. Cook until the steak reaches your desired internal temperature, turning every 5 minutes. Remove once at temp and rest under foil for 10–15 minutes.

Stoke the coals on the hot side to prepare for searing. If you can hold your hand over the coals for longer than 3 seconds, you may have to top up with some freshly lit coals to make sure you have sufficient heat. Sear the steak for 1–2 minutes on each side, then serve immediately.

## SMOKER

Heat a smoker to 135°C (275°F). Pat the steak dry with paper towel and season well with salt. Lay the steak in the smoker to cook until it reaches your desired internal temperature. Remove once at temp and rest under foil for 10–15 minutes.

The steak will need to be seared to finish over a high heat source. This can be a hot grill, a pan on a stove or even a pan placed onto the firebox if hot enough. Sear the steak for 1–2 minutes on each side, then serve immediately.

# TYPES OF SMOKERS

Barbecued smoked meats have a distinct flavour that is seriously addictive, being cooked over very low temperatures in smoky environments until the muscle fibres succumb to tenderness. I myself had a quasi-religious experience the first time I tasted a Texas barbecue beef rib.

There is an inexhaustible variety of smokers on the market, from pit barrel cookers, cabinet water smokers and gravity-fed units all the way through to home-made smokers made from converted filing cabinets or fridges! Restaurants and food service have access to even larger units still, like gas-assisted wood-burning smokers with huge internal rotisseries.

Here, I highlight the most common backyard consumer units available, explain how they work and share my own pros and cons for each type of smoker. What you end up choosing to use at home will largely depend on the space you have available, and the level of effort you are comfortable with.

## THE OFFSET PIT

The most commonly used smoker in Texas, the offset pit is the hardest to master, but produces superior results when used correctly. It's my preferred smoker of choice at home, fired entirely by wood logs with heat control via manual manipulation of the vents. Unlike most other smokers where small amounts of wood are added for flavour, an offset generates both its heat and smoke from whole logs (hence the nickname 'stick burner').

Offsets take a while to get dialled in, are the most labour intensive to run and it takes some practice to get used to controlling the temperature without any spikes. You're also at the mercy of the weather, with cold temperatures, humidity or rain potentially messing with your heat management. For all the effort they take, offsets will produce the best-looking bark (the dark exterior crust), natural smoke rings and meats with a rich, smoky flavour. Plus, an offset gives you full bragging rights.

## CERAMIC EGG COOKERS

Wildly popular and available under a range of different brand names, these egg-shaped cookers are made from ceramic material, which is an incredible insulator and heat retainer. They are very versatile as they allow you to both grill and smoke, although you will have to swap out certain attachments to prepare for different cooking styles.

The smoking is done with a bed of lump charcoal that is laden with wood chunks, and effectively you are cooking on an outdoor oven, similar to a tandoor. The heat source is charcoal, with smoke being added for flavouring. The temperature is controlled by vents, but they are far easier to master than the vents on an offset pit. Smoked meats from a ceramic egg cooker are impressive for a backyard unit, but can have a 'roasted' flavour profile.

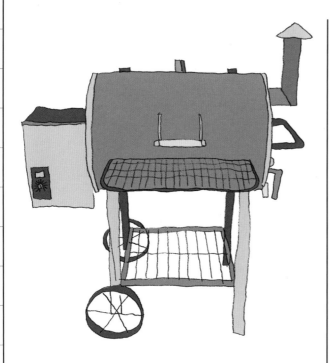

## BULLET SMOKER

Also known as water-pan smokers, these bullet-shaped vertical units are handy for those who don't have a lot of space for a giant smoker, but of course that comes at the sacrifice of the cooking area size—you may have trouble fitting a large brisket in many of them. The water at the base of the unit keeps moisture in the cooking chamber, which can help prevent the meat from drying out.

Much like the grill and ceramic egg, these smokers get their heat from charcoal, so if you want smoke you will need to throw some wood chunks or chips on the coals. Unlike a pellet grill, there aren't many parts on a bullet smoker that can break, but there are quite a few pieces that assemble together to form the unit. That, plus the thin material they are constructed from, means they can lose and leak heat, making it tricky to maintain a constant temperature.

## PELLET GRILLS

If you want a set-and-forget unit without any effort (and, some might argue, skill), a pellet grill is for you because they have in-built thermostats that allow you to set the precise temperature. Pellet cookers are fuelled by compressed wood pellets, which are held in a hopper, pushed along by an auger and ignited to create smoke.

The smoke in these units can be extremely mild, sometimes even requiring a smoker box or tube to amplify the smokiness of the finished food. You'll also need an extension cord and outdoor outlet—these grills run on electricity, and lots of internal mechanisms make for pricey repairs if something goes wrong.

As for the food that pellet grills produce ... Despite being called a grill, most units don't get hot enough to properly sear off a steak.

## ELECTRIC SMOKER

Electric smokers are set-and-forget cabinets with a heating element and a small box for wood shavings. This style of smoker lacks the combustion (and subsequently, creation of specific gases) of any other type of cooker in this guide, and so the meats cooked on them lack a distinct flavour profile. The 'wood' is usually the consistency of sawdust, and smoulders rather than burns clean, which can leave the meat with an acrid taste. They do work and they do produce a form of smoked meat, but they are the least true to the taste and culture of traditional barbecue.

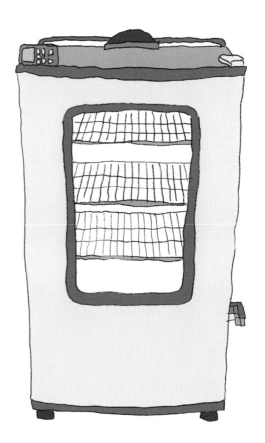

## CHARCOAL GRILL

Don't let the name fool you; the humble charcoal/kettle grill can be converted into a pretty decent smoker. Arranging the coals into a snake configuration (where the coals are stacked around the very edge of the grill and ignited at one end only), and studding them with a few wood chunks, creates a long cook time at low heat that's perfect for barbecuing. However, until you really get the hang of the method, you'll likely have to refill your coals during the cook to get them to last the entire time, which can be awkward. Due to the size of most kettles, there is often a space issue with fitting the meat on the indirect area without it being too close to the heat source.

# THE CARNIVORE'S ARSENAL

These are the essential knives I carry in my knife roll.

## SLICING KNIFE
For briskets, roasts and thinly sliced meats

## CLEAVER
For chopping through joints and smaller bones

**CHEF'S KNIFE**
For all-purpose slicing, cutting, chopping and dicing

**BONING KNIFE**
For trimming, boning and filleting

**PARING KNIFE**
For fine detail trimming and neatening cuts

**BUTCHER'S KNIFE**
For cutting steaks from primals and other large muscle cutting

# HOW TO SPATCHCOCK A CHICKEN

**This rather amusing term refers to the flattening of a chicken or bird to make it level, helping it to cook more evenly.**

**1.** The tools for the job are kitchen shears and paper towel.

**2.** Remove the giblets and any other material from inside the chicken cavity.

Place the chicken on a board, breast side down, and use the kitchen shears to cut up one side of the backbone.

**3.** Snip along the other side of the backbone and remove it completely.

**4.** Flip the chicken over, place a square of paper towel over the breast to prevent any slipping, and push down firmly to break the breastbone and flatten the chicken.

**5.** If you like, you can now tuck the wings under the bird (this will prevent the delicate wing tips from burning).

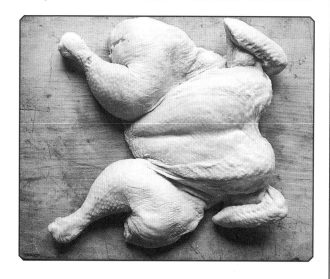

**6.** Your chicken is now spatchcocked and ready to be cooked.

# HOW TO CUT, BUTTERFLY AND TRUSS A LOIN

**Once you get the hang of butterflying a loin, you can use this technique with just about any large whole muscle you'd like to stuff. With a little practice, you'll be creating a lovely even truss in no time.**

**1.** The tools for the job are a boning knife and some butcher's twine (which you can get at good grocery stores and specialty markets, or just ask your friendly butcher).

**2.** Butterflying will take place with three major cuts, which will resemble a very narrow 'U' shape when viewed from the end.

**3.** Make the first cut about 1 cm (½ inch) from the bottom of the loin, stopping before you cut all the way through. For a neat appearance, try to cut in one smooth motion rather than making small cuts.

**4.** Continue your cut, although it will be much shorter, to follow the curve of the loin.

**5.** Make the final cut, which will open up the piece into one even slab.

**6.** Arrange the desired stuffing across the length of the loin.

**7.** Measure and cut a section of twine at least three times the length of the loin.

**8.** Working from left to right, about 2 cm (¾ inch) in from the edge, tie a loop and knot it securely.

**9.** Loop the twine around the loin again, then pass the end of the twine from left to right underneath the loop, pulling to tighten. This should secure the second loop.

**10.** Continue the process, spacing the loops evenly.

**11.** When you reach the end of the loin, knot the final loop on the right side. If you prefer, you can tie one loop at a time and knot it, rather than connecting them in one continuous piece.

(To make this stuffed venison, see page 78.)

# HOW TO GRIND YOUR OWN BURGERS

**Grinding the meat for your own burgers is a great way to not only control their quality, but also experiment with the flavour of different cuts. Brisket, short rib, chuck and round are all great options for grind. They are all tougher cuts that benefit from the grinding to break down the tough fibres. You should not be using any premium cuts like tenderloin or rib eye ... it's just a waste!**

Truth be told, the final fat ratio and texture will have a much bigger part to play in terms of the final taste than the cuts themselves. No matter which combination of cuts you choose, make sure you have at least 20 per cent fat content in your final grind to ensure juicy results.

Whether you use a hand crank or a grinder attachment that fixes to a machine, the most important thing is to keep your equipment and meat cold, and work as quickly as possible. If the fat heats up too much, it will start to smear and affect the texture of the grind.

* Place your grinder in the freezer to cool for at least an hour prior to use.
* Trim the meat of any sinew or connective tissue, and cut it into cubes no larger than 2–3 cm (¾–1¼ inches). Return to the fridge to cool for at least an hour before grinding.
* Working quickly, pass the meat through the grinder to form the minced (ground) meat.
* Place the minced meat back into the fridge for another hour before forming into patties, so that it remains cold and your hands don't melt the fat. Do not add any salt until the cooking process, as this will give your burgers an undesirable texture.

EASY PINK PEPPERCORN AND
RED WINE REDUCTION / PAGE 196

HOME-MADE
BEER MUSTARD
/ PAGE 195

CLASSIC BÉARNAISE / PAGE 196

TRUFFLED BUTTER / PAGE 195

# THE ULTIMATE CONDIMENT SPREAD

Inspired by elegant steakhouse dining, this is my version of a perfect condiment selection to be serving alongside steaks. Having people round for a steak dinner? Let the flavour of the beef speak for itself. Season the steaks simply with salt, then lay out these tasty jams, butters and sauces for an impressive way to let your guests customise their meat.

ONION JAM / PAGE 194

HORSERADISH CRÈME FRAÎCHE / PAGE 197

# HIND
## QUARTER:
## THE RECIPES

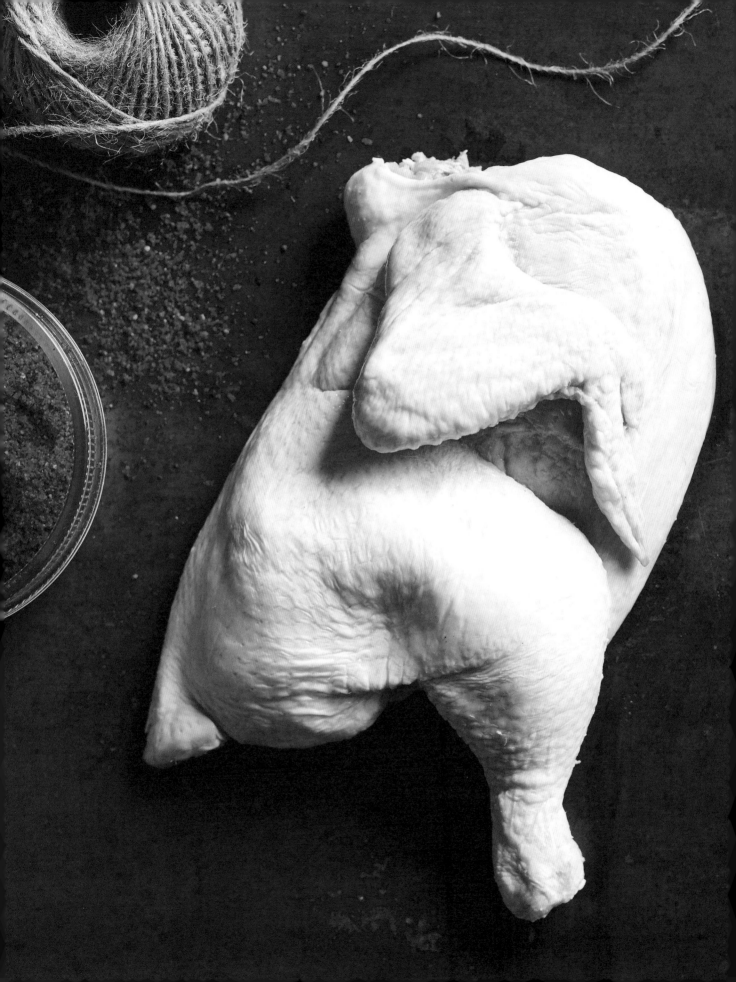

# CHAPTER ONE

## CHICKEN

# PICKLE-BRINED CHICKEN NUGGETS

## SERVES 4-6

Don't throw out that pickle juice—put it to good use! The salty solution adds another layer of flavour and helps retain moisture for a juicier result. Cornflake crumbs are the secret to a super crunchy nugget. If you can't find the crumbs at your local grocery store, you can blitz your own cornflakes in a blender. And if you want something to dip your nuggets in, try the Buffalo dipping sauce (page 202).

### BRINE
375 ml (13 fl oz/1½ cups) pickle juice
1 tablespoon light brown sugar

### NUGGETS
2 boneless, skinless chicken breasts
110 g (3¾ oz/¾ cup) plain
    (all-purpose) flour
¼ teaspoon cayenne pepper
1 teaspoon garlic powder
1 teaspoon freshly ground black pepper
2 teaspoons kosher salt
2 eggs
75 g (2¾ oz/1½ cups) cornflake crumbs
1 teaspoon paprika
1.5 litres (52 fl oz/6 cups) vegetable
    oil, for deep-frying

### METHOD
To make the brine, combine the pickle juice and brown sugar in a bowl, stirring until the sugar has dissolved.

To make the nuggets, cut the chicken into 4 cm (1½ inch) cubes, place in a bowl and cover with the brine solution. Put the bowl in the fridge for 2–4 hours. Remove the chicken pieces from the brine and roughly dry with paper towel.

Prepare your 'crumbing' station with three bowls. In the first bowl, put the flour, cayenne pepper, garlic powder, pepper and salt. In the second, put the two eggs and whisk to combine. In the third, put the cornflake crumbs and paprika.

Pour the vegetable oil into a deep-sided frying pan and place over medium-high heat. Allow the oil to reach 185°C (365°F).

While the oil is heating, take the chicken pieces and roll them first in the flour mixture, then in the egg wash, and finally coat well in the crumb mixture. Place on a large plate. Repeat until all the pieces have been coated.

Add the chicken to the oil in batches, being careful not to overcrowd the pan. Fry for about 4 minutes on each side, then remove and place on paper towel to drain. Allow the oil to come back up to temperature between each batch. Let the nuggets cool slightly before serving.

# POLLO POPPERS

## SERVES 8-10

**Jalapeño poppers are awesome, but the multi-layered bacon wrap doesn't always crisp all the way through. Instead, I like to put the crispy bacon pieces inside the filling along with the shredded chicken. You can prepare these in advance; just hold off the crumbing until you are ready to put them in the oven.**

### METHOD

Preheat the oven to 165°C (330°F). Line a baking tray with baking paper.

Put the cream cheese in a bowl and add the bacon, chicken, cheese, spices and salt. Stir together, combining well.

Slice the jalapeños in half lengthways and remove any seeds and stems. It's advisable to use disposable gloves for this step.

Take a jalapeño half and, using a spoon, scoop in a heaped teaspoon of the cream cheese mixture, spreading the mixture all the way to the sides to form a seal. Don't scrape the cheese mixture flat; leave it slightly mounded to give the crumb something to stick to. Fill the remaining jalapeños with the cheese mixture.

Pour the panko crumbs into a shallow bowl. Press the stuffed side of each jalapeño into the panko to form the coating, then place on the tray with the coating facing up.

Spray lightly with cooking oil and transfer to the oven. Bake for 20-30 minutes, until the panko is just starting to brown and the cheese mixture is softened and warmed all the way through. Remove and allow to cool for at least 5 minutes before serving (the molten cheese centre is hot!).

### INGREDIENTS

250 g (9 oz) cream cheese, softened
8 slices bacon, diced, cooked and cooled
90 g (3¼ oz/½ cup) cooked and shredded chicken
25 g (1 oz/¼ cup) finely grated cheddar cheese
½ teaspoon paprika
½ teaspoon garlic powder
½ teaspoon onion powder
½ teaspoon chipotle powder
1 teaspoon kosher salt
10 large jalapeño chillies
60 g (2¼ oz/1 cup) panko breadcrumbs
cooking oil spray

### CHANGE IT UP

Since all the meat is already cooked, you could grill these jalapeño poppers on the indirect side of a two-zone grill with the lid closed, until the filling has warmed through.

# PEANUT BUTTER AND JELLY WINGS

## SERVES 4-6

It sounds a little strange but, trust me, these flavours will make sense to your tastebuds. The peanut butter creates a rich, thick coating while the jam helps the wings caramelise on the grill. They are an easy way to feed a large crowd, too.

### INGREDIENTS

1 kg (about 2 lb) chicken wings
kosher salt
4 tablespoons strawberry jam
2 tablespoons smooth peanut butter
1 teaspoon sambal oelek
2 tablespoons Worcestershire sauce
2 tablespoons light brown sugar
2 teaspoons paprika
2 tablespoons chopped peanuts

### METHOD

Put the chicken wings in a large resealable plastic bag and season well with salt.

In a bowl, mix together the jam and peanut butter. Add the sambal oelek, Worcestershire sauce, brown sugar and paprika, and mix thoroughly. Pour the marinade into the bag, and massage the bag gently to distribute the marinade over all the chicken wings.

Place the bag in the fridge to marinate for at least 2 hours, or preferably overnight.

Heat a grill to medium. Place the wings on the grill and cook, turning them every 2-3 minutes. This should allow the colour to develop without burning before the chicken is cooked all the way through. Continue to turn the wings until they are nicely browned with charred areas.

Place on a tray to cool slightly. Sprinkle with chopped peanuts for a textural garnish.

### HNOW YOUR CUTS ·

It's better to use wings that have been jointed into wingettes and drumettes. A full three-joint wing will take longer to cook, and the delicate wing tips burn very easily.

# GRIEVEN

**These golden morsels will fast become your new favourite indulgence. A traditional Jewish dish, *grieven* (also called *gribenes*) are a sinfully tasty treat of fried chicken skin 'cracklings' and sautéed onion. Spoon them onto hearty rye or soft challah bread, eat them as is, or stir them through mashed potatoes for a next-level comfort dish.**

## METHOD

Cut the chicken skins into 1–2 cm (½–¾ inch) pieces. You can use kitchen shears to snip them into pieces, which is often easier than using a knife, as the skins can be slippery.

Put the skins, fat and water in a saucepan over medium heat to render. The water will evaporate and the skins will start to brown.

Once the browning has begun and the fat has rendered, add the onion and reduce the heat to low.

Cook, stirring occasionally, until the onions and skins have turned a dark golden brown, and the pieces of chicken skin are crispy. This process, from the time you first start cooking, will take 30–40 minutes.

Pour the mix through a sieve over a bowl, reserving the strained fat. This is known as 'schmaltz', the poultry version of lard or tallow, and can be used for cooking. Store in a jar in the fridge for up to 1 week.

Drain the chicken skins and onion on paper towel, sprinkle with salt and enjoy!

## INGREDIENTS

**225 g (8 oz) chicken skins (with as much fat attached as possible)**
**1 tablespoon chicken fat**
**125 ml (4 fl oz/½ cup) water**
**½ onion, diced**
**kosher salt**

### MASTER THE MEAT
You can ask your butcher for left-over chicken skins, or simply save them up yourself, storing them in the freezer until you have enough to make a batch.

# TORTILLA SOUP

**SERVES 6**

A showcase of classic Mexican and Southwestern flavours, this spicy tomato-based broth gets its name from the fried tortilla strips, which are added to the soup right before serving. If you're feeling particularly lazy or time poor, it's a great one to make in the slow cooker, too.

## INGREDIENTS

80 ml (2½ fl oz/⅓ cup) vegetable oil

5 corn tortillas, cut into thin strips

80 g (2¾ oz/½ cup) diced onion

1 teaspoon garlic powder

1 teaspoon ground cumin

2 teaspoons paprika

1 litre (35 fl oz/4 cups) chicken stock (page 204)

400 g (14 oz) can diced tomatoes

kosher salt

2 boneless, skinless chicken breasts

2 tablespoons cornmeal (fine polenta)

400 g (14 oz) can black beans, rinsed and drained

400 g (14 oz) can corn kernels (or use fresh if you prefer), rinsed and drained

50 g (1¾ oz/½ cup) grated cheddar cheese

25 g (1 oz/½ cup) chopped coriander (cilantro) leaves

1 small avocado, peeled and diced

1 lime, cut into wedges

## METHOD

Heat 2 tablespoons of the vegetable oil in a frying pan over medium-high heat. Add the tortilla strips and fry until golden brown, then remove and drain on paper towel.

Heat the remaining oil in a large pot, then add the onion and cook until browned. Add the garlic powder, cumin and paprika and stir to combine.

Increase the heat to medium-high and add the stock, tomatoes and salt, to taste. Bring to the boil, then add the chicken breasts and cornmeal. Reduce the heat to low and simmer for 15 minutes.

Remove the chicken breasts, shred with a fork, then return the meat to the pot. Add the black beans and corn and simmer for a further 6-8 minutes so everything can warm through. Taste the soup and add more salt if needed.

Place some of the tortilla strips in the bottom of each bowl, reserving some for garnish. Ladle the soup over the strips, then top with the cheese, coriander, avocado chunks and a squeeze of lime. Garnish with the remaining tortilla strips and serve.

## SWAP IT OUT

For a garnish shortcut, use crushed corn chips instead of the fried corn tortilla strips.

# GRILLED ADOBO CHICKEN

### SERVES 8–10

Mexican adobo is a robust marinade made primarily from dried chillies. The Vegemite is an optional ingredient, but it's the secret to my adobo sauce. Although it's considered a breakfast condiment, Vegemite has a salty, umami kick just like beef bouillon, which makes it a perfect savoury flavour booster.

## METHOD

Trim any excess fat or gristle from the chicken thighs. Season well with salt and place in a large bowl.

Remove the stems and seeds from the dried chillies, then put the chillies in a heatproof bowl and pour over just enough boiling water to cover them. Set aside to soak for 5–7 minutes until softened.

Put the chipotle chillies and the sauce from the can in a blender or food processor. Add the dried chillies plus the soaking liquid, the garlic clove, onion, cumin and Vegemite, if using. Blend until smooth.

Pour the blended sauce over the chicken, then use a spatula to mix them well, to ensure they are evenly coated in the sauce. Cover and place the bowl in the fridge for 1 hour.

Heat a grill to medium–high. Once hot, spray the grill grates with oil and place the chicken thighs, skin side down, on the grill and cook for 8–10 minutes on each side, until the internal temperature reads 74°C (165°F).

## INGREDIENTS

2 kg (about 4½ lb) boneless chicken thighs, skin on
kosher salt
2 dried ancho chillies
2 dried guajillo chillies
boiling water
200 g (7 oz) can chipotle chillies (in adobo sauce)
1 garlic clove, peeled
1 onion, roughly chopped
1 teaspoon ground cumin
2 teaspoons Vegemite (optional)
cooking oil spray

GRILLED ADOBO CHICKEN / PAGE 57

# CAJUN BRICK YARDBIRD

## SERVES 4-6

**This is a wonderful method for whole grilled chicken. Spatchcocking the bird ensures a more even cook, while the pressure of the brick pins the skin against the heat source to create crisp, golden skin. This chicken pairs perfectly with Alabama white sauce (page 201) or Louisiana remoulade (page 197).**

## METHOD

Set up a grill for two-zone cooking and heat to medium.

Rinse the chicken well under cold water, removing any giblets and trimming back any excess fat from around the cavity. Pat dry with paper towel.

Spatchcock the chicken (page 34) and place, skin side down, on a foil-lined tray. Drizzle 1 tablespoon of the olive oil over the underside and sprinkle with 1 tablespoon of the Cajun seasoning and massage well. Flip the bird over and repeat with the remaining oil and seasoning, making sure you spread the oil into the crevices between the thighs and wings.

Place the chicken, skin side down, on the indirect heat side of the grill, and place a foil-covered brick on top. You may need to use one brick across the chicken breast and another across the thigh area.

Grill for 25-30 minutes, then turn the chicken over. Replace the bricks, using the opposite (clean) side of the foil to touch the cooked side. Grill for a further 30 minutes, or until a thermometer inserted into the thickest part of the thigh reads 74°C (165°F).

Transfer to a board, cover loosely with foil and rest for 7-9 minutes, then cut into pieces and serve.

## INGREDIENTS

1 x 2-3 kg (about 4½-6½ lb) chicken

2 tablespoons olive oil

3 tablespoons Cajun seasoning (page 209)

---

### MASTER THE MEAT

You will need one or two bricks for this recipe. Make sure you wrap them in foil since they'll be making direct contact with the bird.

# PROSCIUTTO-WRAPPED CHICKEN WITH BROWNED SAGE BUTTER

<u>SERVES 4</u>

Browned butter is one of those sauces that is so easy to create, yet has a huge flavour payoff. I serve any left-over sauce in a ramekin, so my guests can have an extra drizzle or two.

Don't worry if your prosciutto is a little loose, as it shrinks against the chicken during the cook, wrapping it tight and helping to keep the breasts moist. Here, I've paired the dish with the Grilled romaine lettuce from page 185.

## INGREDIENTS

4 boneless, skinless chicken breasts
kosher salt and freshly ground black
    pepper
8 paper-thin slices of prosciutto
2 tablespoons olive oil
90 g (3¼ oz) salted butter
12 sage leaves
2 teaspoons lemon juice

## METHOD

Preheat the oven to 200°C (400°F). Line a baking tray with baking paper.

Season the chicken breasts with salt and pepper. Lay two pieces of prosciutto on a board so they slightly overlap lengthways to create one larger piece, then place a chicken breast on top, positioning it at one end of the prosciutto. Wrap the prosciutto around the chicken and place on the tray, seam side down. Repeat with the remaining chicken and prosciutto. Brush the tops of the wrapped breasts with olive oil.

Place the tray in the oven and cook for 20–25 minutes, until the internal temperature reaches 71°C (160°F).

While the chicken is in the oven, put the butter in a small saucepan over medium-low heat. Cook for about 5 minutes, or until the butter starts to develop a brown colour. Add the sage leaves and lemon juice, reduce the heat to low and continue to gently cook to a deeper brown colour.

To serve, cut the chicken into generous slices and spoon the browned butter on top.

# SUMAC-DUSTED ROAST CHICKEN

## SERVES 4-6

Classic roast chicken receives a zesty upgrade here, with a sprinkle of sumac—a vividly burgundy-hued spice that lends a beautiful colour and a citrus-like freshness. The trick to crispy skin is to dry-brine it—applying salt and leaving the chicken uncovered in the fridge overnight before roasting.

## METHOD

Start this recipe the day prior to serving.

Rinse the chicken well under cold water, removing any giblets and trimming back any excess fat from around the cavity.

Use paper towels to pat the entire chicken dry, then season liberally with salt. Tuck the wings under the bird, then place it, breast side up, into a roasting pan with a rack. The rack keeps air circulating around the bird during cooking, which helps to encourage crispier skin. Leaving it uncovered, put the pan in the fridge overnight, or for at least 8 hours.

When you remove the chicken from the fridge, do everything you can to avoid getting any liquid or water on the skin again—it's this dryness that will help create an awesome skin.

Preheat the oven to 220°C (425°F). Cut the lemon in half again and place into the cavity of the chicken, along with the garlic cloves. Use butcher's twine to truss the legs together, wrapping it around the end of the legs to bring them together. Sprinkle the sumac evenly across the top of the chicken.

Transfer the pan to the oven and roast for 45-60 minutes, until the internal temperature reaches 71°C (160°F). To check this, insert your thermometer between the chicken leg and thigh, making sure not to touch bone (which will give you a false reading). Technically speaking, 74°C (165°F) is the safe temperature for chicken, but it will continue to cook after you remove it from the oven, so we're allowing for that.

Once the chicken has reached the correct temperature, remove from the oven and let it rest for at least 15 minutes before carving.

## INGREDIENTS

1 x 2 kg (about 4½ lb) chicken
kosher salt
½ lemon
2 garlic cloves, peeled
1 tablespoon sumac

### CHANGE IT UP

If you're a serious garlic fan, cut a whole garlic bulb in half and add it to the pan at the same time as the chicken. Once roasted, garlic has a gentle but complex flavour. Squeeze or pull the roasted garlic cloves out of the papery skin and serve with the chicken.

# CHAPTER TWO

# GAME

# COFFEE-RUBBED KANGAROO FILLET

## SERVES 4-6

**Kangaroo is a game meat notorious for being extremely lean, similar to venison. The searing method in this recipe avoids overcooking, while the coffee is a bold complement to any strong, gamey flavours.**

## METHOD

To make the coffee rub, place all the rub ingredients in a bowl and mix well.

Spoon the coffee rub over the kangaroo fillets, making sure they are generously coated. Press the rub into the meat.

Place a frying pan over high heat and add the olive oil. Sear the crusted roo fillets for 3–4 minutes on each side, then remove and allow to rest briefly before slicing and serving.

It's important to serve the kangaroo rare, as it is very tough when overcooked. If you do happen to overcook it slightly, make sure to slice it thinly and against the grain.

## INGREDIENTS

4–5 kangaroo loin fillets
2 tablespoons olive oil

## COFFEE RUB

2 tablespoons ancho chiili powder
2 tablespoons coffee grounds (not powdery, but a very fine grind)
¼ teaspoon cayenne pepper
1 teaspoon ground cumin
½ teaspoon ground coriander
1 teaspoon garlic powder
1 teaspoon mustard powder
2 teaspoons kosher salt
1 teaspoon freshly ground black pepper

# SEARED DUCK BREAST WITH SPIKED FIG SAUCE

## SERVES 2

Unlike chicken, duck can (and should) be served still pink in the middle. The trick to medium-rare duck with super crisp skin is to start off cooking it in a cold pan, and let gentle, persistent heat do its thing.

### INGREDIENTS
2 boneless duck breasts, skin on

### SPIKED FIG SAUCE
175 g (6 oz/1 cup) roughly chopped dried figs, stems removed
250 ml (9 fl oz/1 cup) chicken stock (page 204)
500 ml (17 fl oz/2 cups) dark red wine, such as cabernet
2 tablespoons light brown sugar
1 rosemary sprig
2 tablespoons balsamic vinegar
kosher salt and freshly ground black pepper
1 tablespoon softened unsalted butter
1 tablespoon plain (all-purpose) flour

### METHOD
To make the spiked fig sauce, put the figs, stock, wine, brown sugar and rosemary sprig in a saucepan over medium heat. Simmer until the liquid has reduced by half, then remove the rosemary and discard. Using an immersion or stick blender, blend the figs until smooth. Add the balsamic vinegar, season to taste with salt and pepper, then bring the sauce to the boil.

In a small bowl, mix the softened butter and flour together to form a paste. Whisking constantly, add the paste to the sauce to thicken and create a glossy finish, then immediately reduce the heat to low. If not being used immediately, the sauce can be warmed over a low heat just before serving (take care, as heating it over a high heat may cause it to split).

To prepare the duck, preheat the oven to 180°C (350°F). Pat the duck breasts dry with paper towel, and season well with salt and pepper. Using a sharp knife, score three or four lines across the skin, being careful not to cut into the flesh.

Place the breasts, skin side down, into a cold ovenproof skillet (I use a cast-iron or carbon-steel pan for this) or heavy-based frying pan, and place over low heat. Press down on the duck breasts every minute or so to maximise the skin contact with the pan.

Cook for 8–12 minutes, until the skin is crisp and most of the fat has rendered down. Flip the breasts over and sear for 30 seconds, then turn them back over so they are skin side down again. Transfer the pan to the hot oven and cook for a further 5–6 minutes.

Remove the duck from the oven and place on a board. Cover with foil and allow to rest for 10 minutes before slicing. Serve with a drizzle of the spiked fig sauce over the top.

# CABRITO GUISADO

## SERVES 6-8

*Cabrito* is the Spanish term for young or kid goat, and in South Texas it's commonly prepared asado style: splayed open and cooked over glowing coals. However, the lean meat can dry out very easily, so this *cabrito guisado* (literally, goat stew) is a tasty safe bet for a tender and moist result. Traditional *carne guisada* is just braised meat in sauce, but I like to add in some potatoes and veg to make it a complete meal in a bowl.

## INGREDIENTS

2 tablespoons olive oil

2 kg (about 4½ lb) boneless young goat meat, diced into bite-sized pieces

1 onion, diced

4 garlic cloves, crushed

1 capsicum (bell pepper), diced

1 tablespoon Worcestershire sauce

½ teaspoon ground cinnamon

½ teaspoon ground cumin

1 teaspoon chipotle powder

90 g (3¼ oz/⅓ cup) tomato paste (concentrated purée)

500 ml (17 fl oz/2 cups) beef stock (page 205)

500 ml (17 fl oz/2 cups) water

2-3 carrots, cut into large chunks

3-4 waxy potatoes, cut into large chunks

kosher salt and freshly ground black pepper

## METHOD

Heat 1 tablespoon of the olive oil in a large pot over medium-high heat. Working in batches, add the goat meat and brown on all sides, then remove to a bowl.

Add the remaining oil to the pot, then add the onion, garlic and capsicum and cook for 5-7 minutes, or until softened, scraping up all the browned bits from the bottom of the pot.

Add the meat, Worcestershire sauce, cinnamon, cumin, chipotle and tomato paste, and stir to combine all the ingredients. Pour in the stock and water and bring to the boil, then reduce the heat to a simmer and cover with a lid.

Simmer over low heat for 1½ hours, then add the carrots and potatoes. Season to taste with salt and pepper. Cover again and cook for a further 30 minutes, or until the meat and vegetables are tender.

# QUAIL WRAPS

Traditionally these wraps were made with dove meat, and dove season is a big deal in Texas, being the first of all the hunting seasons to open. Quail is a delicious alternative and is available year round. A Texan once told me his final dying meal would be as many of these morsels as he could eat in one sitting.

## METHOD

Set up a grill for two-zone cooking and heat to medium.

Rinse the quail breasts under cold water to clean them, remove the breast plate if still intact, then cut them in half, separating the lobes. Season well with salt.

Cut the bacon strips in half widthways. If the strips are too long and wrap around the quail too many times, the bacon will not crisp during cooking.

Put the cream cheese in a bowl and add the garlic powder, onion powder and pepper. Stir together, combining well.

Slice the jalapeños in half lengthways and remove any seeds and stems. It's advisable to use disposable gloves for this step.

Take one jalapeño half and, using a spoon, fill the hollow with the cream cheese mixture. Place one of the quail breast halves on top, and wrap the whole parcel in a strip of bacon, securing it with a toothpick. Repeat until all the wraps are assembled.

Place the wraps on the indirect heat side of the grill. Cook, turning every 2–4 minutes, until the bacon is crisp. If your bacon is not getting crisp enough, you can place the wraps directly over the heat for 20–30 seconds at a time, but be careful to avoid flare-ups from the grease dripping onto the coals. Remove the toothpicks and serve.

## INGREDIENTS

6 whole, deboned quail breasts
kosher salt
6 slices streaky bacon
175 g (6 oz) cream cheese, softened
1 teaspoon garlic powder
1 teaspoon onion powder
1 teaspoon coarsely ground black pepper
6 jalapeño chillies

QUAIL WRAPS / PAGE 73

# VENISON CHILI

## SERVES 6-8

No self-respecting Texan (even an honorary variety like myself) would ever put beans in their chili. Instead of using the express version, which calls for a powdered chilli blend, this chili is made using soaked and toasted dried chillies, resulting in an intense and complex sauce.

## METHOD

Place a frying pan over medium-high heat. Add the ancho, guajillo and árbol chillies and toast for 30 seconds on each side, until pliable and fragrant. Remove from the pan and, when cool enough to handle, pull the stems off and tip the seeds out.

Put the toasted chillies in a small saucepan, pour in the stock and simmer over low heat for 5-10 minutes, until soft. If the stock doesn't just cover the chillies, add a little water.

Put the stock, softened chillies, canned chipotle chillies and garlic in a food processor. Process until smooth.

Heat half the olive oil in a large pot over high heat. Working in batches, add the venison to the pot and brown on all sides. Remove and set aside.

Add the remaining oil to the pot and cook the onion for about 7 minutes, or until softened, scraping up all the brown crispy bits from the venison off the bottom of the pot. Add the cumin, cinnamon and salt and stir to combine.

Return the meat to the pot and add the puréed chilli sauce, beer, vinegar and brown sugar. Reduce the heat to low, then cover and simmer for 1 hour.

Add the cornmeal to the pot and continue cooking for a further 10-15 minutes, until the meat is tender and the sauce has reduced and thickened, coating the venison pieces.

## INGREDIENTS

3 dried ancho chillies
2 dried guajillo chillies
2 dried chiles de árbol
500 ml (17 fl oz/2 cups) beef stock (page 205)
3 chipotle chillies (canned in adobo sauce)
3 garlic cloves, peeled
60 ml (2 fl oz/¼ cup) olive oil
1 kg (about 2 lb) diced venison
1 onion, diced
2 teaspoons ground cumin
1 teaspoon ground cinnamon
2 teaspoons kosher salt
250 ml (9 fl oz/1 cup) beer (pilsner or lager style)
1 tablespoon apple cider vinegar
1 tablespoon light brown sugar
2 tablespoons cornmeal (fine polenta)

# PECAN AND CRANBERRY STUFFED VENISON BACKSTRAP

## SERVES 6-8

There's some technical skill needed to butterfly meat and prepare it for stuffing (see page 36 for a step-by-step guide), but you'll get better each time you try. Once all your elements are prepared, this dish comes together very quickly—it's ready in just 15 minutes.

## INGREDIENTS

75 g (2¾ oz/¾ cup) pecans
75 g (2¾ oz/½ cup) dried cranberries
5 thyme sprigs
2 French shallots, diced
3 tablespoons dried breadcrumbs
¼ teaspoon ground nutmeg
¼ teaspoon freshly ground black pepper
½ teaspoon kosher salt, plus extra for seasoning
60 g (2¼ oz) butter, melted
1 whole venison backstrap (about 1 kg/2 lb)
2 tablespoons olive oil

## METHOD

Toast the pecans in a frying pan without any oil until fragrant, stirring regularly to avoid burning. Roughly chop the nuts and put in a bowl.

Chop the cranberries and add to the bowl, then strip the thyme sprigs and add the leaves to the bowl, discarding the woody stems. Add the shallots, breadcrumbs, nutmeg, pepper and ½ teaspoon salt. Stir to combine the ingredients. Add the melted butter and stir again until everything is well mixed.

Butterfly or fillet the backstrap so it's flat and even. Form the pecan and cranberry stuffing mixture in a log lengthways down the middle. Pull the backstrap back together to form a cylinder around the stuffing, and secure with butcher's twine. Season the outside well with salt.

Preheat the oven to 180°C (350°F). Heat the olive oil in an ovenproof frying pan over high heat until nearly smoking. Add the stuffed backstrap and sear for about 2 minutes on each side, until browned all over.

Place the pan in the oven and cook for a further 4-6 minutes for perfect rare, or up to 10 minutes for something closer to medium. It's important not to overcook the backstrap or it will become tough.

Remove the venison from the pan, cover loosely with foil and set aside to rest for 8-10 minutes before slicing into 2.5 cm (1 inch) thick portions.

## MASTER THE MEAT

If you're having trouble getting the hang of trussing, you can buy food-safe elasticised bands, which you simply slip around the stuffed loin at different intervals to hold in place.

# DUCK FAT HUMMUS WITH GRILLED FLATBREADS

### SERVES 4-6

Duck fat has a very mild flavour that is almost neutral, but gives a rich, silky texture to the hummus dip. You can omit the sour cream from the dough recipe if you want to keep it dairy free.

## DUCK FAT HUMMUS

320 g (11¼ oz/2 cups) canned or
    cooked chickpeas (garbanzo beans)
90 g (3¼ oz/⅓ cup) tahini
2 tablespoons duck fat
1 large garlic clove, peeled
60 ml (2 fl oz/¼ cup) lemon juice
½ teaspoon ground cumin
½ teaspoon kosher salt, plus extra
    to taste
125 ml (4 fl oz/½ cup) water
1 tablespoon olive oil
1 teaspoon paprika or sumac

## FLATBREADS

2 teaspoons instant dry yeast
1 teaspoon sugar
185 ml (6 fl oz/¾ cup) warm water
300 g (10½ oz/2 cups) plain
    (all-purpose) flour
2 tablespoons sour cream
1 tablespoon olive oil, plus extra
    for brushing
½ teaspoon kosher salt

## METHOD

To make the duck fat hummus, drain and rinse the chickpeas and put in a blender or food processor. Add the tahini, duck fat, garlic, lemon juice, cumin, salt and half the water. Pulse on high until smooth.

Taste and add more salt if necessary. If the hummus is too dry, add the remaining water in small increments until you reach the desired consistency. Scrape into a bowl, cover and set aside.

To make the flatbreads, combine the yeast, sugar and warm water in a bowl. Leave the mixture to bloom for 12 minutes.

Add the flour, sour cream, olive oil and salt. Stir to combine and then knead for 5-7 minutes. I find it easiest to do this using the dough hook attachment of an electric stand mixer, but if you don't have one, tip the mixture onto a lightly floured work surface and knead the dough with your hands for 7-10 minutes, or until the dough is smooth and elastic. Cover with a cloth and place in a warm spot to rise for 1 hour.

Divide the dough in half, then divide each half again into thirds, giving you a total of six portions. Using a rolling pin, roll out each piece until they are no thicker than 5 mm (¼ inch).

Heat a grill to medium. Brush one side of the flatbread with a little olive oil, then place on the hot grates. While it's cooking, brush the other side with oil. Cook for 2 minutes on each side, taking care not to burn the bread. If space allows, you can grill several flatbreads at a time.

Drizzle the hummus with the olive oil and sprinkle with paprika or sumac, then serve with warm flatbreads.

### CHANGE IT UP
Instead of a grill, you can use a cast-iron skillet or comal (a Mexican griddle) on the stovetop to cook the flatbreads.

# SMOKED 'N' SPICED VENISON JERKY

## SERVES 6-8

Venison is the perfect protein candidate to be transformed into jerky because it's naturally lean. Although you can use a dehydrator to make jerky, you'll probably never turn back once you've tried it smoked. I prefer to use pecan or robustly flavoured woods like hickory or mesquite. You'll need to start this recipe ahead of time to allow time for freezing and marinating the venison.

## METHOD

Put the venison in the freezer for 45–60 minutes to make slicing easier. Remove from the freezer and cut the meat into thin strips, no thicker than 5 mm (¼ inch).

Combine all the remaining ingredients in a large resealable plastic bag. Add the meat and massage the bag gently to distribute the marinade over all the meat. Place in the fridge overnight, or for at least 6 hours.

Prepare a smoker to cook at 65°C (150°F).

Remove the meat from the marinade and pat down with paper towel, trying to remove as much moisture as possible.

Lay the venison strips in the smoker and smoke until they are completely dried out. There is no set time for this, as it depends on the size of the slices, the temperature of the smoker, the humidity and the weather, but generally this will take at least 8 hours or so.

Jerky strips will have the longest shelf life if you can vacuum-seal them after drying, otherwise store them in an airtight container and store in the fridge or cupboard for up to 7 days.

## INGREDIENTS

1 kg (about 2 lb) venison (see Tip)
125 ml (4 fl oz/½ cup) soy sauce
2 tablespoons Worcestershire sauce
2 tablespoons light brown sugar
2 tablespoons hot sauce (ready-made or see page 202)
1 teaspoon onion powder
1 teaspoon garlic powder
1 teaspoon freshly ground black pepper
1 teaspoon chilli flakes
½ teaspoon cayenne pepper
½ teaspoon ground cumin
2 teaspoons kosher salt
60 ml (2 fl oz/¼ cup) water

### KNOW YOUR CUTS

You can use any type of venison cut for jerky; just make sure all the sinew and silver skin is trimmed away. Since backstrap is one of the few larger muscles, you're better off saving it for more exciting recipes. I prefer to use meat from the leg or shoulder.

# RABBIT AND ANDOUILLE GUMBO

## SERVES 6-8

A stew as dark and murky as the Louisiana swamps it hails from, gumbo comes in many variations, the protein combinations traditionally dictated by whatever was trapped or caught that day. The key to a good gumbo is a complex roux base—the darker, the better.

## METHOD

Heat 1 tablespoon of the olive oil in a large pot over medium heat and brown the sausage on both sides. Remove from the pot and set aside.

Season the rabbit pieces on both sides using half the Cajun seasoning. Add another tablespoon of oil to the pot. Working in batches, add the rabbit and brown on both sides. Remove and set aside.

Add the final tablespoon of oil to the pot, then add the 'trinity'—the onion, celery and capsicum—plus the garlic. Cook for 5-7 minutes to soften the vegetables, stirring and picking up all the browned bits from the bottom of the pot. Add the bay leaves, cayenne pepper and remaining Cajun seasoning.

Meanwhile, heat the stock in a small saucepan and bring to a gentle simmer.

Add the roux to the pot with the onion mixture and stir well to combine everything. Add one ladle of warm stock to the roux mixture, stirring as you pour it in. Continue to add one ladle of stock at a time until all the stock is incorporated.

Bring the mixture to the boil, then return the rabbit and sausage to the pot. Discard any excess fat that has accumulated from the sausage and do not pour it back into the pot (the fat will pool on the surface).

Reduce the heat to low, cover with a lid and simmer for 45-60 minutes, until the rabbit is tender. Remove the rabbit pieces from the pot and pick the meat off the bones. Return the meat to the pot, discarding the bones. Make sure you remove the rabbit pieces before the meat is completely falling off the bone; rabbit has some very small bones that may end up in the finished gumbo if you leave it cooking for too long.

Increase the heat to a vigorous simmer, then add the hot sauce. Cook for a further 5 minutes to warm the rabbit pieces. Serve in bowls ladled over boiled rice.

## INGREDIENTS

60 ml (2 fl oz/¼ cup) olive oil
350 g (12 oz) andouille sausage, cut into large pieces
1 rabbit, cut into large pieces
1½ tablespoons Cajun seasoning (page 209)
1 onion, diced
3 celery stalks, diced
1 green capsicum (bell pepper), diced
2 garlic cloves, minced
2 bay leaves
1 teaspoon cayenne pepper
1.5 litres (52 fl oz/6 cups) chicken stock (page 204)
1 batch of roux (page 153)
2 tablespoons hot sauce (ready-made or see page 202)
boiled white rice, to serve

### SWAP IT OUT

If you can't find andouille (which is a Cajun smoked sausage), you can substitute with good-quality chorizo or another smoked pork sausage.

# DUCK LIVER PARFAIT WITH SHIRAZ JELLY

## SERVES 4

I used to think parfait (a smoother, silkier version of pâté) was a complicated and laborious dish that only chefs should tackle, but it's actually fairly easy to make at home. The shiraz wine is an Aussie twist on the traditional port jelly, which seals the surface of the parfait.

### PARFAIT
400 g (14 oz) duck livers
125 g (4½ oz) unsalted butter
4 thyme sprigs
1 bay leaf
1 French shallot, finely diced
2 tablespoons brandy
50 ml (1¾ fl oz) thickened
   (heavy) cream
¼ teaspoon ground nutmeg
¼ teaspoon kosher salt

### JELLY
2 tablespoons water
1½ teaspoons unflavoured
   powdered gelatine
185 ml (6 fl oz/¾ cup) shiraz
2 teaspoons sugar

### METHOD
To make the parfait, trim the livers of any sinew, keeping the globes as intact as possible.

Place a frying pan over medium-low heat. Add 1 tablespoon of the butter, 3 thyme sprigs and the bay leaf, then add the shallots and cook until softened. Discard the herbs and use a slotted spoon to remove the shallots to a food processor.

Return the pan to high heat, letting it warm up, then add the livers. Cook for about 1 minute on each side, crusting the outsides but ensuring the middles are still pink. Add the brandy and flambé until the alcohol is cooked off, then add the livers to the food processor. Pulse to blend until smooth.

Add the cream, nutmeg and salt to the processor and pulse again to combine. Add the remaining butter, then pulse a final time to blend to a smooth mousse.

Pass the mixture through a fine sieve or chinois into a serving dish. Refrigerate for 30-45 minutes until set.

To make the jelly, put the water in a small heatproof bowl and sprinkle the gelatine over the top. Allow to sit for 3-4 minutes.

Meanwhile, warm the shiraz and sugar in a small saucepan over low heat until the sugar has just dissolved. Pour onto the gelatine mix and stir until the gelatine has completely dissolved. Allow to cool slightly.

Gently pour the jelly over the parfait. Delicately press the remaining thyme sprig into the still-liquid jelly for decoration, then return to the fridge to set for at least 1 hour before serving.

### CHANGE IT UP
The parfait is delicious slathered onto slices of fresh sourdough that have been brushed with a little oil and grilled.

# TURKEY AND DUMPLINGS

### SERVES 6-8

The classic Southern soup/stew hybrid is usually made with chicken, but turkey is a perfect alternative, particularly at certain times of the year when you may have left-over turkey meat filling your fridge. The 'dumplings' are pillowy clouds of pepper-spiked dough, which make for a hearty winter meal.

## METHOD

To make the stew, melt the butter in a large saucepan over low heat, add the flour and mix to combine. Stir for a minute or so to cook out the flour, then add a cup of the stock and whisk to combine. Add another cup, then whisk again until all the lumps are gone. Pour in the remaining stock.

Increase the heat and bring the mixture to a simmer, then add the carrots and celery and cook until softened. Add the shredded turkey and bring to the boil.

To make the dumplings, combine all the ingredients in a bowl. Stir a few times to combine, but do not overwork the dough.

Use a scoop or spoon to drop balls of dumpling dough into the boiling stew, then place a lid on the pan and reduce the heat to low. Cook the dumplings for 7-9 minutes, or until puffed up and cooked through. Remove the lid and serve.

## STEW

125 g (4½ oz) butter
75 g (2¾ oz/½ cup) plain (all-purpose) flour
2 litres (70 fl oz/8 cups) chicken stock (page 204) or turkey stock
3 carrots, diced
2 celery stalks, diced
250-375 g (9-13 oz/2-3 cups) cooked shredded turkey

## DUMPLINGS

150 g (5½ oz/1 cup) plain (all-purpose) flour
1 teaspoon baking powder
½ teaspoon kosher salt
1-2 teaspoons coarsely ground black pepper
60 ml (2 fl oz/¼ cup) milk
2 tablespoons butter, melted

---

### SWAP IT OUT

For an even richer dumpling, substitute the butter with rendered chicken or turkey fat.

# VENISON SKILLET BAKE

## SERVES 6-8

**Gooey, melty, cheesy, meaty. This all-in-one pasta bake is comfort food in its purest form, and guaranteed to have you considering a second helping.**

### INGREDIENTS
500 g (about 1 lb) spiral pasta
2 tablespoons olive oil
1 large onion, diced
1 garlic clove, minced
500 g (about 1 lb) minced (ground)
    venison
1 teaspoon kosher salt, or to taste
700 ml (24 fl oz) passata
    (puréed tomatoes)
1 teaspoon dried oregano
1 handful of basil leaves, julienned
75 g (2¾ oz/¾ cup) grated
    cheddar cheese
100 g (3½ oz/¾ cup) grated
    mozzarella cheese

### METHOD
Preheat the oven to 180°C (350°F). Cook the pasta according to the directions on the packet, draining the pasta 1-2 minutes before the recommended cooking time. The pasta should be a bit firmer than *al dente*. Set aside.

Using the pot from the pasta, heat the olive oil over medium heat. Add the onion and garlic and cook until the onion is softened. Add the venison, season with the salt and cook until browned, stirring with a wooden spoon to break up any lumps.

Stir in the passata, oregano and basil and cook for a further 2-3 minutes. Add the cooked pasta, half the cheddar and half the mozzarella. Stir well to incorporate and then pour everything into a 30 cm (12 inch) ovenproof cast-iron skillet.

Top with the remaining cheeses. Transfer to the oven and bake for 25-30 minutes, or until the cheese is bubbly and golden brown.

### SWAP IT OUT
If you don't have a cast-iron skillet, you can prepare the filling in a large saucepan and then transfer everything to a casserole dish before baking.

# CHAPTER THREE

# PORK

# BLT SALAD WITH BACON-FRIED CROUTONS

### SERVES 4

As the saying goes, you don't make friends with salad ... unless that salad has bacon in it. After pan-frying the bacon, the rendered fat is used to toast the croutons to a state of salty, porky goodness, then the whole salad is finished with a mayo vinaigrette.

## INGREDIENTS
6 slices streaky bacon
2–3 thick slices sourdough bread,
    cut into 2 cm (¾ inch) cubes
1 head butter lettuce
2–3 large ripe tomatoes
1 tablespoon snipped chives
2 teaspoons freshly ground black
    pepper
kosher salt
2 tablespoons mayonnaise
1 tablespoon white wine vinegar
1 teaspoon wholegrain mustard

## METHOD
Cut the bacon strips into three or four pieces and place in a frying pan over medium heat. Cook for about 15 minutes, or until crisp. Remove using a slotted spoon and place on paper towel to drain.

Increase the heat to medium-high, then add the bread cubes to the hot bacon grease. Cook for 3–5 minutes, turning to brown all sides, until golden. Remove using the slotted spoon and place on paper towel to drain.

Cut the core off the lettuce and separate the leaves. Wash and dry the lettuce leaves, then roughly tear the leaves and arrange on a platter. Slice the tomatoes and scatter them over the lettuce. Arrange the croutons and bacon on top, then sprinkle with the chives, pepper and salt, to taste.

In a small bowl, combine the mayonnaise, vinegar and mustard. Season with salt and whisk to combine. Drizzle the vinaigrette over the salad before serving.

## MASTER THE MEAT
This is a great recipe to feature your own home-made bacon (page 117), cut as thin or chunky as you'd like.

# BRAZILIAN CHEESY PUFFS WITH PANCETTA

These light cheese puffs are a meat-laden version of traditional Brazilian *pão de queijo*, and texturally are like an airy, chewy savoury marshmallow. My secret is to add crispy pancetta—it's the non-smoked counterpart of bacon and matches well with the delicate flavour of the puffs.

## METHOD

Preheat the oven to 200°C (400°F). Place a shallow frying pan over medium-low heat and cook the diced pancetta for 10-15 minutes, or until the fat has rendered and the pancetta turns crispy. Drain the pieces well and place on paper towel to soak up the extra grease.

Combine the milk, vegetable oil and salt in a small saucepan over medium heat. Slowly heat until the mixture is just about to boil, but do not allow it to boil.

Add the tapioca flour to the heated milk mixture and stir to combine, then pour the mixture into the bowl of a stand mixer. Using the paddle attachment, mix on medium speed for 5 minutes, or until the dough has begun to form.

Add the eggs and continue to beat for a further 2 minutes. Add the parmesan and gruyère cheeses and the cooled pancetta and mix until just combined.

Use a mini ice cream scoop to scoop small balls of the mixture into a 24-hole mini muffin pan. You can also use a baking tray lined with baking paper, but make sure you leave space between each mound of dough.

Bake for 20-25 minutes, until the dough has puffed and is just starting to turn golden. Remove from the oven and allow to cool for a few minutes before serving.

## INGREDIENTS

125 g (4½ oz) pancetta, diced
250 ml (9 fl oz/1 cup) milk
80 ml (2½ fl oz/⅓ cup) vegetable oil
1 teaspoon kosher salt
225 g (8 oz/2 cups) tapioca flour
2 eggs, lightly whisked
45 g (1½ oz/½ cup) grated
    parmesan cheese
50 g (1¾ oz/½ cup) grated gruyère
    cheese

### CHANGE IT UP
This recipe calls for a stand mixer, but if you don't have one you can do the stirring by hand; however, the sticky tapioca flour will require some serious elbow grease.

# BLUE CHEESE, DATE AND BACON BITES

MAKES 12

Some recipes demonstrate that just a few carefully matched ingredients can create something utterly more-ish (and this is one of them!). Use a firmer blue cheese (rather than a brie-based one) as it will be easier to handle and less likely to seep out of the dates during cooking.

## INGREDIENTS
75 g (2¾ oz) firm blue cheese
6 slices streaky bacon
12 pitted medjool dates

## METHOD
Preheat the oven to 200°C (400°F). Line a baking tray with baking paper.

Slice the blue cheese into rectangular cubes, about as long as the dates in length and about 5 mm (¼ inch) wide. Cut each slice of bacon in half.

Using a paring knife, slit each date down one side to open it up, place the blue cheese block inside, then pinch to close back up.

Take one of the cut strips of bacon and roll it around the date, securing with a toothpick, then place on the tray. Repeat the process until all the dates have been stuffed and wrapped. Put the tray in the oven and bake for 7–10 minutes, until the bacon has crisped.

## CHANGE IT UP
You can grill these bites instead of oven roasting; just soak the toothpicks in water for 30 minutes before use, to help prevent them catching and burning.

# BARBECUED PULLED PORK SANDWICHES

### MAKES 12

This is real deal barbecued pork, which traditionally uses Boston butt, a cut from the top part of the shoulder. The meat is rubbed with spices and smoked at low heat until it's pull-apart tender, then combined with a tangy barbecue sauce to create a sensationally porky sammich. This recipe makes twelve generous sandwiches, and you'll have some left-over pulled pork, too. If you can't find pork butt for this recipe, use shoulder, collar or scotch.

## METHOD

Prepare a smoker to cook at 105°C (225°F). During the cook, you'll want to hold the temperature between 105°C (225°F) and 120°C (250°F).

Trim the pork butt of any excess fat and sinew. Apply the dry rub to all surfaces of the pork, making sure it's well coated. Use your hands to massage it into the butt (yes, I said it).

Place the pork butt in the smoker and cook until the meat reaches an internal temperature of 93-96°C (200-205°F), spritzing with apple juice every 90 minutes. The meat should be extremely tender, with no resistance to a temperature probe or knife being inserted. This may take anywhere from 6 to 10 hours.

If you are having trouble with a 'naked cook', you can speed up the process and buy some 'extra moisture insurance' by wrapping the butt tightly in foil after it's had about 3 hours of smoke exposure. Return the wrapped pork to the smoker to cook until the internal temperature hits between 93°C (200°F) and 96°C (205°F). Remove the pork once at temperature, cover with foil and rest for 30-60 minutes.

Place the butt in a roasting pan or large dish. Use your hands or two forks to pull the meat apart.

Cut each burger bun in half and layer a generous handful of the pulled pork on the bun bases, top with a few tablespoons of KC barbecue sauce and a scoop of slaw, then place the bun top on the pile. Serve immediately.

## INGREDIENTS

1 x 2.5-3 kg (about 5½-6½ lb) pork butt

75 g (2¾ oz/½ cup) Pork season-all dry rub (page 209)

500 ml (17 fl oz/2 cups) apple juice (in a spray bottle)

12 soft burger buns

250 ml (9 fl oz/1 cup) Kansas City-style barbecue sauce (page 200)

Tangy vinegar slaw, to serve (page 174)

### CHANGE IT UP

If you don't have a smoker, you can create pulled pork in a slow cooker. Add 500 ml (17 fl oz/ 2 cups) of chicken stock to the bottom of the slow cooker, then add the pork and cook on low for 6-8 hours until fall-apart tender. It will be super yummy, but remember: it's only true barbecue if you smoke it!

BARBECUED PULLED PORK SANDWICHES / PAGE 95

# CHAR SIU SKEWERS

### SERVES 4-6

One could argue that the Chinese were one of the original practitioners of barbecue, and their traditional char siu sticky and sweet barbecue sauce makes a heck of a partner for pork. Serve with Sambal bok choy (page 184) for a spicy side to balance the sweet.

**INGREDIENTS**

1 kg (about 2 lb) boneless pork shoulder or neck, cubed
1 tablespoon crushed garlic
1 tablespoon finely chopped fresh ginger
2 tablespoons soy sauce
2 tablespoons hoisin sauce
1 tablespoon oyster sauce
1 tablespoon shaoxing rice wine
3 tablespoons sugar
90 g (3¼ oz/¼ cup) honey
½ teaspoon Chinese five spice
½ teaspoon kosher salt
4-6 drops red food colouring

**METHOD**

Put the pork, garlic and ginger in a large resealable plastic bag or sealable container.

In a small saucepan, combine the soy, hoisin and oyster sauces, rice wine, sugar, honey, five spice, salt and red food colouring. Place over medium heat and stir until the sugar has melted, then remove the pan from the heat and allow the mixture to cool.

Once the marinade has cooled, pour it over the pork in the bag, mixing well to make sure all the pieces are coated. Place in the fridge to marinate overnight.

Heat a grill to medium. Thread the pork cubes onto skewers, then place onto the grill and cook for 10-12 minutes, until cooked through, turning the skewers every 2-3 minutes to prevent burning.

# SPICY GOCHUJANG BARBECUE BABY BACK RIBS

## SERVES 2

Baby back ribs are usually associated with Memphis-style barbecue, but these ribs are bathed in smoke before being mopped with gochujang—a spicy, fermented, funky and sweet Korean sauce, which is sometimes sold as a paste. Note that if you do use the paste, you'll need to dilute the consistency to be thinner, and you can do this by adding water until it is the consistency of ketchup or tomato sauce. For a less-spicy version, you can swap the gochujang with Sweet rib glaze (page 210).

## INGREDIENTS

1 rack baby back pork ribs

3 tablespoons Pork season-all dry rub (page 209)

2 tablespoons butter

60 g (2¼ oz/¼ cup, firmly packed) light brown sugar

125 ml (4 fl oz/½ cup) gochujang sauce

## METHOD

Prepare a smoker to cook at 105°C (225°F).

Prepare the ribs. Start by trimming any extra fat away, and removing the membrane from the back of the bones (just loosen the corner of the membrane with a butter knife, then use a paper towel to grip and pull the membrane away).

Use a paper towel to pat the ribs dry, then season generously with the dry rub on both sides. Set aside for 10–15 minutes so the ribs 'sweat' and the rub becomes a paste.

Place the ribs in the smoker for 3 hours, making sure to monitor and maintain your 105°C (225°F) temperature without any major spikes or drops.

Prepare two large squares of foil, one on top of the other, and put the butter and brown sugar along the bottom. Remove the ribs from the smoker and place the ribs, meat side down, onto the butter and sugar. Wrap the parcel tightly and return to the smoker for a further 1 hour.

After the hour has passed, carefully open the foil package (there may be quite a bit of liquid that has accumulated), remove the rack and gently return it to the smoker, bone side down. If this is too difficult, you can simply unwrap the ribs and tuck the foil in at the sides, forming a 'boat' around the meat, leaving the tops of the ribs exposed.

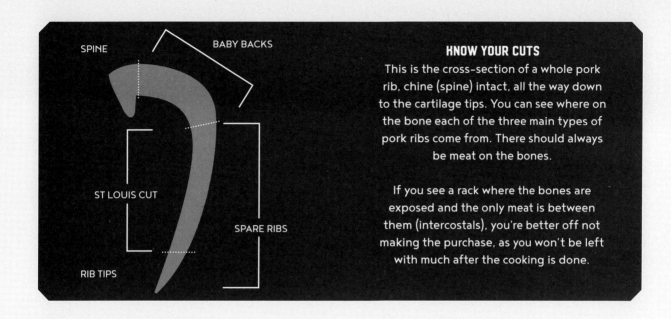

SPINE

BABY BACKS

ST LOUIS CUT

SPARE RIBS

RIB TIPS

## KNOW YOUR CUTS

This is the cross-section of a whole pork rib, chine (spine) intact, all the way down to the cartilage tips. You can see where on the bone each of the three main types of pork ribs come from. There should always be meat on the bones.

If you see a rack where the bones are exposed and the only meat is between them (intercostals), you're better off not making the purchase, as you won't be left with much after the cooking is done.

Using a pastry brush, paint a generous amount of the gochujang sauce onto the meat side of the rack. Close the lid and smoke for a further 15–20 minutes, which will allow time for the sauce to gel and set. You should be able to lightly tug on the bones and feel little resistance. If you feel they could be more tender, leave them in the smoker for up to an hour extra, basting them again with the sauce if desired.

SPICY GOCHUJANG BARBECUE BABY BACK RIBS / PAGE 100

# SEARED LOIN WITH SOUR CHERRY CHUTNEY

## SERVES 6-8

**Use the guide on page 36 to learn how to expertly cut a loin to get it ready for stuffing, giving it a huge 'wow' factor when it hits the table. The chutney is rich and fragrantly spiced, with the perfect hint of sweetness.**

## METHOD

To make the sour cherry chutney, put the dried cherries in a small bowl, then add enough boiling water to just cover. Leave to soak for 5–7 minutes until softened, then drain.

Put the cherries, onion, vinegar, cinnamon stick, cloves, brown sugar, ginger, tarragon, mustard seeds and orange zest and juice in a saucepan. Place over medium heat, cover with a lid and simmer for 12–15 minutes. Remove the lid and continue to simmer until the liquid has evaporated and the mixture has thickened to a jammy consistency. Remove from the heat and allow to cool.

Trim the pork loin of any excess fat. Sometimes there will be a thick fat cap that should be trimmed back, so only a thin 2–3 mm (about ⅛ inch) layer remains. Slice the loin open to allow for stuffing, then spoon 4–6 tablespoons of the chutney down the middle of the loin. There should be enough chutney to form a log about 4 cm (1½ inches) in diameter.

Gently roll the loin back up, and then truss with butcher's twine to secure the shape.

Preheat the oven to 200°C (400°F). Season the entire outside of the loin well with salt and pepper.

Place a large ovenproof frying pan on the stove over high heat. Once the pan is hot, add the loin and sear for 1–3 minutes, then turn the loin over and repeat until all sides are seared.

Place the pan in the oven and cook until the meat reaches an internal temperature of 61°C (142°F). Remove from the oven, place the loin on a board and cover loosely with foil. Allow the pork to rest for 10–15 minutes. Cut and remove the trussing, then slice into 2–3 cm (¾–1¼ inch) rounds and serve.

## INGREDIENTS

1 kg (about 2 lb) pork loin roast
kosher salt and freshly ground black pepper

### SOUR CHERRY CHUTNEY

200 g (7 oz/1¾ cups) dried cherries (unsweetened)
boiling water
150 g (5½ oz/1 cup) diced red onion
250 ml (9 fl oz/1 cup) apple cider vinegar
1 cinnamon stick
4 whole cloves
100 g (3½ oz/½ cup, lightly packed) light brown sugar
55 g (2 oz/¼ cup) diced crystallised (glacé) ginger
2 tablespoons chopped tarragon
1 teaspoon mustard seeds
zest and juice of 1 orange

### SWAP IT OUT
If you can't find tart dried cherries, you can use regular or frozen cherries instead—just skip the rehydration step.

# CIDER-BRINED PORK CHOPS WITH MUSTARD SAUCE

## SERVES 4

Apple and pork are complementary flavours, so it makes sense to start them mingling well in advance of the cooking. The secret to chops with a beautiful crust that are still tender and juicy on the inside is to start the brining process the night before.

**INGREDIENTS**
4 thick centre-cut bone-in pork chops
2 tablespoons olive oil

**BRINE**
1 litre (35 fl oz/4 cups) apple cider
1 bay leaf
6 allspice berries
65 g (2¼ oz/¼ cup) kosher salt
60 ml (2 fl oz/¼ cup) maple syrup

**MUSTARD SAUCE**
65 g (2¼ oz/¼ cup) American (yellow) mustard
2 tablespoons wholegrain mustard
1 tablespoon apple cider vinegar
2 teaspoons chopped tarragon
1 tablespoon Worcestershire sauce
1 tablespoon maple syrup
½ teaspoon freshly ground black pepper
pinch of kosher salt

**METHOD**
To make the brine, combine all the ingredients in a small saucepan over low heat until the salt has dissolved. Allow the mixture to cool.

Put the pork chops in a dish and pour the cooled brine over the top. Weight the meat down with a plate if necessary. Cover with plastic wrap and place in the fridge overnight.

Preheat the oven to 190°C (375°F). Heat the olive oil in an ovenproof frying pan over high heat. Remove the chops from the brine, pat dry with paper towel and place into the hot pan. Sear the chops for 2–3 minutes on each side, then transfer the pan to the oven to finish cooking. Cook until the meat reaches an internal temperature of 60°C (140°F).

While the meat is cooking, make the mustard sauce. Combine all the sauce ingredients in a small saucepan and heat gently until warmed through. Serve the pork chops drizzled with the mustard sauce.

# SAGE AND MACADAMIA SAUSAGE ROLLS

**These are a more adult version of a classic sausage roll; you can either cut them into party-sized pieces or leave them as longer logs for a meal-worthy feed. The macadamia nuts should be chopped small enough to combine well into the mix, but large enough to still have some crunch.**

## METHOD

Pour the olive oil into a small saucepan over medium heat. Add the onion and garlic and cook for 5-7 minutes until softened, then remove from the heat and set aside.

Preheat the oven to 190°C (375°F). Line a baking tray with baking paper. Remove the puff pastry from the freezer and thaw until pliable.

In a bowl, combine the sage, mustard powder, celery salt, paprika, salt, pepper, macadamias, breadcrumbs, pork and cooled onion mix. Use your hands or a wooden spoon to mix gently until combined.

Place a sheet of puff pastry on a lightly floured board. Take half the pork mix and form it into a log, placing it 3-4 cm (1¼-1½ inches) in from the edge, across the entire width of the pastry sheet. Roll the pastry over to encase the meat completely. Brush some egg wash along the pastry seam and seal the pastry together by pressing gently along the seam with your fingers. If there's excess pastry, use a paring knife to trim it away. Repeat with the second sheet of puff pastry and the remaining pork.

Using a large, sharp knife, cut each log into seven or eight pieces. Put the pieces on the lined tray and brush the tops with the remaining egg wash. Place the tray in the oven and bake for 35-45 minutes, until golden brown. Allow to cool for 5 minutes, then serve with a generous bowl of ketchup.

## INGREDIENTS

**2 tablespoons olive oil**

**1 onion, finely diced**

**2 garlic cloves, minced**

**2 puff pastry sheets**

**1 tablespoon chopped sage (fresh works best but you can use dried)**

**1 teaspoon mustard powder**

**1 teaspoon celery salt**

**1 teaspoon paprika**

**2 teaspoons kosher salt**

**1 teaspoon freshly ground black pepper**

**95 g (3¼ oz/¾ cup) chopped macadamia nuts**

**40 g (1½ oz/⅓ cup) dried breadcrumbs**

**1 kg (about 2 lb) minced (ground) pork (do not use lean)**

**35 g (1¼ oz/¼ cup) plain (all-purpose) flour (or enough to flour a board)**

**1 egg, lightly whisked**

CARNITAS / PAGE 112

# CARNITAS

**SERVES 6-8**

You can find pork carnitas at any decent taco trailer in Texas. The pork is first slow cooked until tender before being rendered down in its own fat to create a more-ish crust flecked with crunchy pork nuggets. This version uses a cheat's method—crisping the meat under an oven grill (broiler)—but the results are equally delicious. You can serve these with tortillas, coriander (cilantro) and a squeeze of lime for instant tacos.

## INGREDIENTS

1 teaspoon olive oil

2 garlic cloves, crushed

1.5 kg (about 3 lb) boneless pork shoulder, cut into 6-8 large chunks

1 tablespoon kosher salt

2 teaspoons freshly ground black pepper

½ teaspoon cayenne pepper

1 teaspoon ground cumin

zest and juice of 1 orange

250 ml (9 fl oz/1 cup) chicken stock (page 204)

## METHOD

Heat the olive oil in a large pot over medium heat. Add the garlic and cook for 3-4 minutes until browned. Add the pork pieces in a single layer, then sprinkle on the salt, pepper, cayenne pepper, cumin and orange zest. Pour in the orange juice and stock.

Reduce the heat to a low simmer, then cover and cook for about 2 hours, or until the pork is pull-apart tender. Using two forks, shred the pork pieces. There should be a combination of smaller shreds and larger chunks for texture.

Heat the oven grill (broiler) to high. Line a baking tray with baking paper.

Use kitchen tongs to remove the shredded pork from the pot, and arrange in a single layer on the tray. Place under the hot grill for 8-12 minutes, to brown and crisp up the pork. Keep an eye on it to ensure it doesn't burn. Toss the pork to combine, taste and add more salt if needed, then serve immediately.

# SALT-CRUSTED CRISPY PORK BELLY

## SERVES 6-8

**Pork crackling is perhaps one of life's greatest pleasures. This method uses the moisture-extracting qualities of salt to achieve a supremely crisp crust.**

## METHOD

Combine the soy sauce, shaoxing wine, garlic, ginger, honey, star anise, cloves and peppercorns in a shallow dish large enough to fit the pork belly.

Using paper towel, pat down the skin of the belly. It's very important to keep the skin as dry as possible from this point on, making sure no moisture or liquid touches it. Carefully place the belly in the marinade, which should come up the sides of the meat, but not touch the skin. Place in the refrigerator, uncovered, overnight.

Preheat the oven to 180°C (350°F). Line a roasting pan with foil to catch any drips. Place a roasting rack on top of the foil, and pour the water into the pan.

Remove the pork belly from the marinade. Scrape off any aromatics that have stuck to the meat and put them in the water (to create a fragrant steam). Place the belly on the rack, skin side up. If the belly is not even, use some scrunched up foil underneath the meat to level it.

Pour the salt onto the skin to form a thick layer. Spread the salt all the way to the edges, making sure the skin is not visible (use extra salt if needed); the salt will turn into a solid crust during cooking. Place in the oven and cook for 40 minutes.

Remove the pan from the oven and increase the oven temperature to 240°C (460°F). Carefully lift off the solid salt crust and discard. Use a pastry brush to brush away any stray salt granules. Return the pork to the hotter oven for 35-45 minutes, to crisp the skin. If the skin hasn't completely transformed to crackling, turn on the oven grill (broiler) and blast it for 10 minutes, keeping a close eye on it to make sure it doesn't burn. Remove and place on a board. Use a cleaver or roast slicer to cut into chunks. Serve immediately.

## INGREDIENTS

125 ml (4 fl oz/½ cup) light soy sauce
60 ml (2 fl oz/¼ cup) shaoxing rice wine
2 garlic cloves, roughly chopped
4-6 cm (1½-2½ inch) piece of fresh ginger, roughly chopped
2 tablespoons honey
3-4 star anise
1 teaspoon cloves
1 tablespoon sichuan peppercorns
1 kg (about 2 lb) piece of pork belly, skin on
185 ml (6 fl oz/¾ cup) water
390 g (13¾ oz/1½ cups) kosher salt

### KNOW YOUR CUTS

Try to select the most even and straight piece of belly for this recipe; it makes a big difference to ensuring all the skin puffs into crackling.

SALT-CRUSTED CRISPY PORK BELLY / PAGE 113

# HOME-MADE BACON

## MAKES ABOUT 1.5 KG (ABOUT 3 LB)

There's something wholly satisfying about making your own bacon, if for no other reason than to be in complete control of how thickly you slice it! You'll need to get your hands on some Prague powder #1 (also known as pink curing salt) for this recipe; it's crucial to the curing phase. There are several types of curing salts, and they are not the same as Himalayan pink salts, which get their colour from natural minerals, so make sure you end up with the salt specifically for 'quick' curing.

## METHOD

The first step is to cure the belly, and this will take a week. Line a baking tray with foil and place the pork belly on top.

In a small bowl, combine the salt, pepper, brown sugar and curing salt. Sprinkle half the dry salt mix on one side of the pork belly, massaging it in well. Flip the pork over and repeat on the other side with the remaining mix.

Put the entire belly into a large resealable plastic bag and place in the fridge for 7 days. Over time, the salt mix will transform into a liquid. Each day, flip the bag over and massage the contents around for 30–60 seconds.

At the end of the 7 days, remove the belly and rinse well under water. Pat dry with paper towel. Put the pork on a rack over a pan (to catch the drips), then return to the fridge, uncovered, for 24 hours.

Prepare a smoker to cook at 95°C (200°F), fuelled with the wood chunks. Once at temperature, place the belly in the smoker and smoke until the internal temperature reaches 65°C (150°F)—this will take about 3 hours.

Once cured with smoke, allow to cool, then store in an airtight container or bag in the fridge for up to 1 week, cutting and cooking as required.

## INGREDIENTS

- 1.5 kg (about 3 lb) boneless, skinless pork belly
- 3 tablespoons kosher salt
- 2 tablespoons freshly ground black pepper
- 75 g (2¾ oz/⅓ cup, firmly packed) light brown sugar
- 1 teaspoon pink curing salt (Prague powder #1)
- wood chunks, chips or logs (depending on your smoker)

### PICKING THE RIGHT WOOD FOR SMOKING

Different woods have different flavour and aroma profiles and change the final taste of your bacon. Fruit woods, such as apple, cherry or plum, traditionally pair well with pork and have a sweeter finish. For a punchier smoke flavour, try mesquite or hickory.

# CHAPTER FOUR
# LAMB

# DUKKAH-CRUSTED BACKSTRAP

## SERVES 4-6

Middle Eastern dukkah is a chunky spice mix, usually flecked with sesame seeds and crushed nuts. I like to use pistachios in mine, and the finished crust creates a great texture with every bite.

### INGREDIENTS

150 g (5½ oz/1 cup) pistachio nuts
135 g (4¾ oz/1 cup) skinless hazelnuts
40 g (1½ oz/¼ cup) sesame seeds
2 tablespoons coriander seeds
1 tablespoon cumin seeds
4 lamb backstraps (about 750 g/
    1½ lb in total)
kosher salt and freshly ground black
    pepper
1 tablespoon honey
1 tablespoon pomegranate molasses
2 tablespoons olive oil

### METHOD

Preheat the oven to 180°C (350°C). Put the pistachio nuts and hazelnuts on a baking tray and toast in the oven for about 5 minutes, or until fragrant. Keep an eye on them to ensure they don't burn. Remove from the tray and set aside.

Toast the sesame, coriander and cumin seeds in a small frying pan (without oil) over medium heat until fragrant, swirling the pan to keep the seeds from burning. Remove from the pan and allow to cool slightly.

Pour the nuts and seeds into a food processor and pulse five or six times until the mixture resembles small breadcrumbs. Don't overwork the mix, as the nuts will begin to release their oils. The dukkah should be dry and not at all moist.

Season the backstraps well with salt and pepper. Combine the honey and pomegranate molasses in a bowl. Pour the dukkah onto a large plate. Working with one backstrap at a time, brush the molasses mix onto the lamb, then roll it in the dukkah.

Heat the olive oil in a frying pan over high heat. Add the backstraps and brown for 1-2 minutes on each side. Be gentle when turning the straps to keep the crust intact.

Place the browned backstraps on a baking tray, then transfer the tray to the oven to finish cooking. Cook until the lamb reaches an internal temperature of 57°C (135°F), which will take 10-15 minutes. Remove from the oven, cover loosely with foil and rest for 5-7 minutes before slicing and serving.

# LAMB PASTRAMI

## SERVES 8-10

Corned in brine and then smoked, this lamb leg pastrami is amazing sandwiched between some rye, with a generous slather of mustard and slices of sour pickles. Pink curing salt (also known as Prague powder #1) is essential to help the meat cure and to retain a pink colour; it's not the same as pink-coloured rock or river salt, so make sure you get your hands on the right product. You'll need to start this recipe three or four days ahead, to allow time for the lamb to cure in the brine and then dry in the fridge.

## METHOD

To make the brine, put the water, sugar and salt in a saucepan and heat until the sugar and salt have dissolved. Remove from the heat and allow to cool completely.

If the lamb is trussed, cut the string away and then place the lamb into a non-reactive bowl or very large resealable plastic bag. Add the curing salt, garlic cloves, pickling spice and juniper, if using. Pour the cooled brine mix over the lamb, ensuring the meat is totally covered in the liquid. Cover the bowl or seal the bag, then place in the fridge to brine for 3 days.

After brining, remove the lamb from the liquid and rinse well. Re-truss or tie the lamb into a ball shape, which will make slicing easier. Place the lamb on a clean tray and return to the fridge, uncovered, for 1 day. If you must skip the extra uncovered drying step, you can, but make sure the lamb is still rinsed after removing from the brine.

Prepare a smoker to cook at 105-120°C (225-250°F).

To make the rub, combine all the ingredients in a small bowl. Sprinkle the rub mix generously over the lamb, pressing it in and ensuring it's well coated.

Smoke the lamb until it reaches an internal temperature of 74°C (165°F), then remove and allow to cool completely. Cut into thin slices to serve.

## INGREDIENTS

1.5 kg (about 3 lb) whole boneless lamb leg

### BRINE

2 litres (70 fl oz/8 cups) water
110 g (3¾ oz/½ cup) sugar
130 g (4½ oz/½ cup) kosher salt
2 teaspoons pink curing salt (Prague powder #1)
2 garlic cloves, peeled
3 tablespoons Pickling spice (page 206)
2 teaspoons crushed juniper berries (optional)

### RUB

2 tablespoons coarsely ground black pepper
1½ tablespoons crushed coriander seeds
1 teaspoon mustard powder
1 teaspoon finely ground dried rosemary

# NEKKID SAUSAGES WITH MINT AND PISTACHIO

## SERVES 8–10

Part skinless sausage, part exotic meatball, these 'nekkid' sausages are inspired by Balkan *cevapi* and Middle Eastern kofta. The fresh herbs and onions provide a bright contrast to the fatty lamb. Prepare and shape these in advance, and grill once ready. You can even make them football shaped for a game-day appropriate feed.

### INGREDIENTS

35 g (1¼ oz/¼ cup) pistachio nuts
1 kg (about 2 lb) minced (ground) lamb
25 g (1 oz/½ cup) chopped mint
15 g (½ oz/½ cup) chopped flat-leaf
   (Italian) parsley
80 g (2¾ oz/½ cup) finely diced onion
1 garlic clove, crushed
2 teaspoons ground cumin
kosher salt
260 g (9¼ oz/1 cup) Greek yoghurt
2 tablespoons lemon juice

### METHOD

Toast the pistachio nuts in a dry frying pan over low heat for 4–6 minutes until fragrant. Transfer to a board and chop the pistachios into small coarse crumbs. (If your pistachios are already toasted, you can skip this step.)

Put the pistachios, lamb, half the mint, half the parsley, onion, garlic and cumin in a bowl. Use your hands to combine all the ingredients, being cautious not to overwork the meat. Take a handful of meat at a time and form the mixture into sausages, about 10 cm (4 inches) in length.

Heat a grill to medium–low. Immediately before grilling, season the sausages well on both sides with a generous sprinkling of salt. Place the sausages on the grill and cook, turning every 5 minutes, until the sausages are browned and have reached an internal temperature of 71°C (160°F).

Put the remaining mint and parsley in a blender or food processor. Add the yoghurt and lemon juice, season with a little salt, to taste, and blend until well combined. Serve the cooked nekkid sausages with the yoghurt dipping sauce.

# LAMB CUTLETS WITH SMOKED ROSEMARY SALT

## SERVES 6-8

The trick to achieving a perfectly pink lamb chop is to cook the cutlets as a complete rack, then slice into chops after resting. Pair these with Charred brussels sprouts (page 181).

## METHOD

Preheat the oven to 180°C (350°F). Place the lamb racks on a board. Rub 1 tablespoon of the olive oil over each rack, then sprinkle with the cumin, salt and pepper.

Place an ovenproof frying pan on the stove over high heat. Working with one lamb rack at a time to avoid overcrowding the pan, sear the lamb for about 2 minutes on each side. Remove and repeat with the second rack.

Return both racks to the pan, then transfer to the oven to finishing cooking. Cook until the lamb reaches an internal temperature of 54°C (130°F), which will take 10–14 minutes. As soon as it reaches temperature, remove the pan from the oven and place the racks on a board. Cover with foil and rest for 5–7 minutes.

To serve, slice the racks into single or double bone chops, then drizzle with a little fresh lemon juice and sprinkle with the rosemary salt.

## INGREDIENTS

2 Frenched lamb racks, fat cap off, about 500 g (about 1 lb) each
2 tablespoons olive oil
2 teaspoons ground cumin
3 teaspoons kosher salt
3 teaspoons freshly ground black pepper
1 lemon, halved
Smoked rosemary salt (page 213)

### MASTER THE MEAT

A Frenched bone is one that is exposed and cleaned, like we see on lamb cutlet racks. Sometimes the bones aren't as neat and clean as we'd like them to be. An easy way to clean them up is to use the string hack. Simply create a loop with some butcher's twine, start at the base of the bone and pull up —any residual meat will be scraped away by the twine.

# SMOKED LAMB SHOULDER

<u>SERVES 6-8</u>

Lamb is practically built for smoking, particularly the tough shoulder with all of its connective tissue and fatty seams. I cook it until tender, then chop it much like whole hog barbecue—going to town with two cleavers on a cutting board! I've paired it here with Jalapeño cornbread (page 189), and you can also serve it with one of the three regional barbecue sauces on pages 200-201.

## INGREDIENTS

2 kg (about 4½ lb) boneless square-cut lamb shoulder

4-6 tablespoons Basic brisket rub (page 206)

## METHOD

Prepare a smoker to cook at 105°C (225°F). The cooking time will take between 7 and 10 hours.

Pat the surface of the lamb dry with paper towel. Apply the rub liberally, pressing it into the meat and making sure it's well coated with an even crust.

If you have a wireless thermometer, insert the probe into the thickest part of the shoulder. It's the easiest way to keep track of the internal temperature without constantly opening your smoker.

Smoke the lamb until the thickest part registers an internal temperature of 91°C (195°F) for chopped lamb, or 99°C (210°F) for pulled lamb.

Once at temperature, remove from the smoker, wrap in foil or butcher's paper and rest for at least 30-45 minutes before chopping or pulling the meat.

### TASTE OF TEXAS

It may seem overly simple, but the basic brisket rub that I like to use on most of my smoked red meats is a hallmark of classic Central Texas-style barbecue. The simplicity of the salt and pepper complements the meat, rather than overpowering it.

# LAMB AND BARLEY STEW

## SERVES 6

This is a serious winter-warmer and a meal-in-a-bowl favourite.
Though not a traditional ingredient, I add shiitake mushrooms
to give this dish an extra boost of umami goodness.

### INGREDIENTS

50 g (1¾ oz) dried shiitake mushrooms
boiling water
2 tablespoons olive oil
1 kg (about 2 lb) boneless lamb pieces,
    cubed
kosher salt and freshly ground black
    pepper
1 onion, diced
3 large carrots, peeled and cut into
    2 cm (¾ inch) pieces
6 thyme sprigs
2 bay leaves
200 g (7 oz/1 cup) pearl barley
500 ml (17 fl oz/2 cups) beef stock
    (page 205)
4 waxy potatoes, cut into large chunks

### METHOD

Preheat the oven to 180°C (350°F). Put the shiitake mushrooms
in a bowl and pour in boiling water until just covered. Set aside
to soak.

Heat the olive oil in a large pot over medium–high heat.
Season the lamb well with salt and pepper. Working in batches,
add the lamb to the pot and brown on all sides. Remove with a
slotted spoon and set aside.

Add the onion, carrots, thyme sprigs and bay leaves to the
pot and cook for 10 minutes, or until the onions have softened.

Drain the liquid from the shiitakes into the pot, then slice the
mushrooms and add them too, along with the lamb, barley and
stock. Stir to combine everything and bring to a simmer.

Put the potato chunks on top of the stew and cover the
pot. Transfer to the oven and braise for 1½ hours, or until the
potatoes and meat are tender.

# GRILLED LAMB RIBS WITH MOLASSES

Pigs aren't the only animals with a rib cage! Lamb ribs are delicious and super easy to grill. You can also use riblets for this recipe, which are from the front or cranial end of the rib cage, and if you get a slab with the breast or belly still on, that will cook up great too, with extra crispy bits to gnaw at.

## METHOD

Place the lamb racks on a large tray and season well with salt and pepper on both sides. Use a pastry brush to paint the molasses onto both sides of the ribs, then use a spatula to spread on the garlic. Cover and place in the fridge for a minimum of 4 hours to marinate.

Set up a grill for two-zone cooking and heat to medium-high. Place the lamb racks on the indirect heat side, and throw the rosemary sprigs directly onto the hot coals to create smoke (see Tip). Close the lid and grill for 30 minutes, or until the fat has begun to render down, making sure to turn the racks over every 5 minutes or so.

If additional colouring is required, stoke the coals to create additional heat, then immediately place the ribs over the direct heat and sear for 2–4 minutes on each side, until a nice char has developed.

Remove the racks from the grill, cover with foil and rest for 10 minutes before slicing and serving.

## INGREDIENTS

2 racks lamb ribs, about 700 g (1½ lb) each
kosher salt and freshly ground black pepper
175 g (6 oz/½ cup) molasses
4 garlic cloves, crushed
6–8 large rosemary sprigs

## SWAP IT OUT

If you use a gas grill, just throw the rosemary sprigs in with the lamb while it's marinating, then discard the sprigs before cooking.

GRILLED LAMB RIBS WITH MOLASSES / PAGE 131

# ROAST LEG OF LAMB WITH LEMONY SHALLOT BUTTER

Leg of lamb should be cooked to medium-rare so it still retains its pinkness, and a roast is about as classic as it comes for this cut. The lamb is seasoned with Greek-inspired flavours complemented by an easy lemon and shallot sauce that's bright and acidic, and helps to cut through the richness of the lamb.

## METHOD

Preheat the oven to 200°C (400°F). If the lamb leg is trussed or in netting, remove the strings and unroll the leg. Spread the crushed garlic all over the inside of the lamb leg, and season generously with salt. Roll the leg back up and replace the netting, or truss it with twine to close it back up in a roll.

In a small bowl, combine the garlic powder, onion powder, oregano, nutmeg, cinnamon and pepper. Drizzle the olive oil over the entire leg and then massage the spice mix all over. Season well with salt.

Put a wire rack inside a roasting pan, and pour in enough water to line the bottom of the pan, but not touch the bottom of the rack. Place the lamb leg on the rack and transfer to the oven. Cook until the meat reaches an internal temperature of 57°C (135°F), which will take about 1½ hours.

Remove the roast once at temperature, loosely cover with foil and rest for 10-15 minutes.

While the lamb is resting, make the lemony shallot butter. Combine all the ingredients in a small saucepan and cook over low heat for 5-10 minutes, stirring occasionally, until the butter has melted and the sauce has combined. Cut the lamb into thin slices and drizzle with the lemony sauce. Serve immediately.

## INGREDIENTS

1 x 1.5-2 kg (about 3-4½ lb) boneless lamb leg
2-4 garlic cloves, crushed
kosher salt
2 teaspoons garlic powder
2 teaspoons onion powder
2 teaspoons dried oregano
½ teaspoon ground nutmeg
½ teaspoon ground cinnamon
1 teaspoon freshly ground black pepper
2 tablespoons olive oil

### LEMONY SHALLOT BUTTER

60 ml (2 fl oz/¼ cup) extra virgin olive oil
1 large French shallot, finely diced
60 g (2¼ oz) butter
zest and juice of 1 lemon
½ teaspoon kosher salt
¼ teaspoon freshly ground black pepper
½ tablespoon chopped oregano

### MASTER THE MEAT

Seasoning the inside of the lamb leg will create a deeper layer of flavour, but if your leg comes already trussed, you can skip the garlic stuffing.

# BALSAMIC BLACKBERRY LAMB SHANKS WITH CREAMY GRITS

## SERVES 4

Shanks are a phenomenal cut for slow cooking. The long braise results in meltingly tender meat, and the rich braising liquid is put to good use as a base for a vivid sauce. If you can't find grits, use polenta (or fine cornmeal) instead; prepare it according to the packet instructions.

## INGREDIENTS

4 lamb shanks
kosher salt
2 tablespoons olive oil
1 onion, diced
2 carrots, diced
300 g (10½ oz/3 cups) frozen blackberries
125 ml (4 fl oz/½ cup) balsamic vinegar
6 cloves
6 cardamom pods (or 2 teaspoons ground cardamom)
1 cinnamon stick
2 thyme sprigs
500 ml (17 fl oz/2 cups) red wine
500 ml (17 fl oz/2 cups) chicken stock (page 204)
45 g (1½ oz/¼ cup, lightly packed) light brown sugar
90 g (3¼ oz/¼ cup) honey
1 tablespoon cornflour (cornstarch)
2 tablespoons butter

## GRITS

500 ml (17 fl oz/2 cups) milk
500 ml (17 fl oz/2 cups) water
155 g (5½ oz/1 cup) white grits
60 ml (2 fl oz/¼ cup) thickened (heavy) cream
2 tablespoons butter

## METHOD

Preheat the oven to 160°C (320°F). Season the lamb shanks generously with salt. Heat 1 tablespoon of the olive oil in a large pot and, working in batches, brown the shanks over high heat. Remove and set aside.

Add the remaining oil to the pot, then add the onion and carrots and cook for 4–6 minutes until softened. Add the blackberries, balsamic vinegar, cloves, cardamom, cinnamon stick, thyme sprigs, wine and stock. Bring the mixture to the boil.

Return the shanks to the pot, laying them on their sides. Cover with a lid and cook in the oven for 1 hour. Uncover the pot, turn the shanks over and cook for a further 45 minutes, uncovered.

Remove the pot from the oven and ladle out some of the braising liquid through a sieve until you have 500 ml (17 fl oz/ 2 cups) of strained liquid. Place this in a small saucepan. Turn the shanks once more in the pot, return to the oven and cook, uncovered, for a final 45 minutes, or until tender.

Add the brown sugar and honey to the strained liquid in the saucepan. Bring to a simmer and cook until reduced by at least half. Dissolve the cornflour in 1–2 tablespoons water, then add this paste and the butter to the sauce, whisking to combine. The finished sauce should have a syrupy consistency.

To make the grits, heat the milk and water to just before boiling. Stir in the grits and cook over low heat, stirring often, for about 20 minutes, or until cooked through and tender. Stir in the cream and butter and season with salt, to taste.

To serve, spoon a generous portion of grits into a bowl and top with a shank. Drizzle a few spoonfuls of sauce over the top. If you want to stretch the meat to feed more people, shred it from the bone and serve shredded portions over the grits.

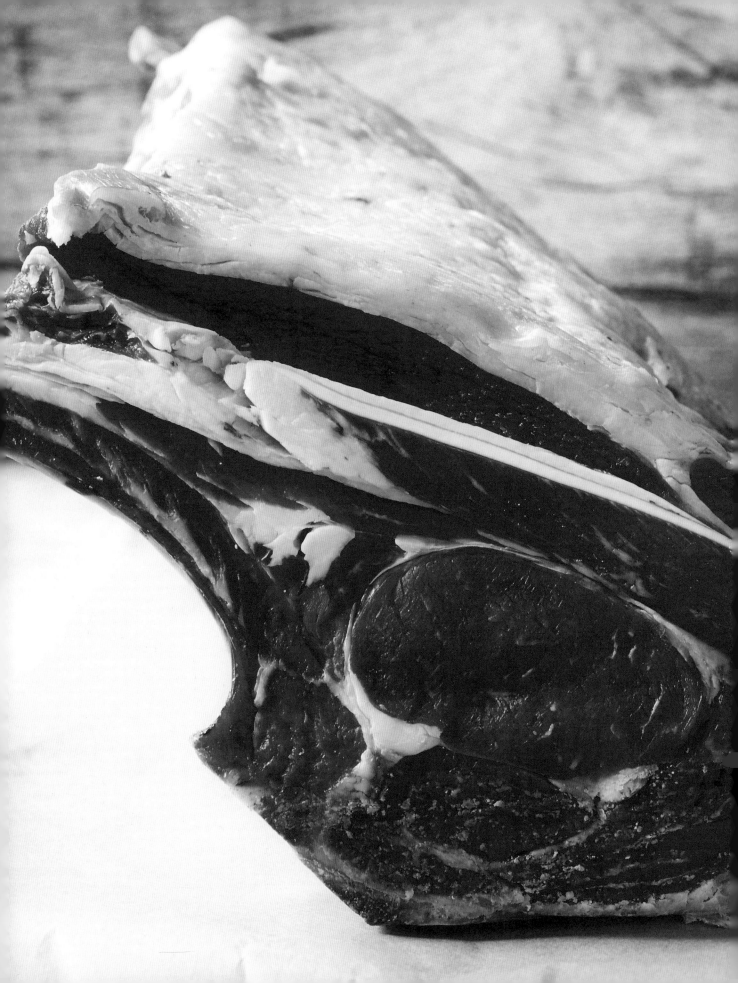

# CHAPTER FIVE

# BEEF

# STEAK AND EGG TACOS WITH HOME-MADE HOT SAUCE

## SERVES 6

Flank steak is perfect for this application—it's a flavoursome cut with a very pronounced grain that is sliced into thin strips to serve. These self-saucing tacos come courtesy of a deliciously runny egg yolk, which mingles with the hot sauce to coat the steak pieces. If you don't want to make your own hot sauce, use any store-bought variety, such as Tabasco, Cholula or Louisiana.

## INGREDIENTS

1 x 1 kg (about 2 lb) flank steak
kosher salt
60 ml (2 fl oz/¼ cup) vegetable oil
6 eggs
6 flour tortillas
1 handful coriander (cilantro) leaves, chopped
Home-made hot sauce, to taste (page 202)
1 lime, cut into wedges

## MARINADE

2 tablespoons olive oil
2 tablespoons red wine vinegar
1 tablespoon Worcestershire sauce
90 g (3¼ oz/¼ cup) honey
1 garlic clove, crushed
1 teaspoon smoked paprika
½ teaspoon ground cumin

## METHOD

To make the marinade, combine all the ingredients in a small bowl. Season the steak generously with salt, then place in a dish or resealable plastic bag. Pour the marinade over the steak, making sure it's well coated, then cover the dish or seal the bag and place in the fridge for 2–4 hours.

Heat a grill to high. Remove the meat from the marinade, shaking off any excess, and cook the steak, turning every 4–5 minutes, until it reaches an internal temperature of 54°C (130°F). Transfer to a board, cover with foil and set aside. While the steak rests, cook the eggs.

Heat the vegetable oil in a frying pan over medium-high heat. Once hot, crack the eggs into the pan, cooking two or three at a time so you don't overcrowd the pan. Working quickly after each egg hits the hot oil, use a spatula to gently push the edges of the whites back towards the yolk, to keep their shape. Cook for 2–4 minutes, until the whites are fried and just set but the yolk is still runny (the runny yolk will act as a sauce). Transfer the fried eggs to a paper towel to absorb some of the oil.

Slice the steak against the grain into 1 cm (½ inch) thick strips. Place two or three meat strips on a tortilla, then top with a fried egg, a sprinkle of coriander, a few dashes of hot sauce and a squeeze of lime.

## MASTER THE MEAT

It's important to always cut flank steak against the grain. Cutting in the other direction will leave you with long tougher strands that are difficult to bite through.

# PETITE TENDER WITH CHIMICHURRI

## SERVES 4

Discovering a lesser known cut can make you feel like the Indiana Jones of the meat world! The petite tender is one of my favourite steak cuts and the fresh Argentinian chimichurri is a great complement.

## METHOD

To make the chimichurri, wash and dry all the herbs, chop roughly, then place in a food processor. Add the chilli, garlic cloves, lemon juice and salt. Process until everything is combined well and the herbs are finely chopped. You want to make sure that you do the majority of the blending before the oil goes in. If you process the mixture too much when adding the oil, it may start to emulsify and make the final sauce cloudy.

With the motor running on medium speed, drizzle in some of the olive oil until the mixture combines. Turn the processor off and pour in the remaining oil. There should be oil present on the spoon when you spoon your chimichurri out, so add additional oil if it appears too dry. Set aside.

Heat a grill to high. Season the petite tenders well with salt. Spray the grill grate with oil, then place the meat directly over the coals and cook, turning every 2 minutes, until it reaches an internal temperature of 54°C (130°F). Transfer to a board, cover loosely with foil and rest for 10 minutes.

After the meat has rested, slice it against the grain into 2 cm (¾ inch) thick slices. Serve with the chimichurri spooned over the top.

## CHIMICHURRI

1 large handful flat-leaf (Italian) parsley leaves
1 large handful coriander (cilantro) leaves
1 small handful oregano leaves
4–5 thyme sprigs (leaves only)
1 mild to medium heat red chilli, roughly chopped
2–3 garlic cloves, peeled
juice of 1 lemon
2 teaspoons kosher salt, or to taste
60 ml (2 fl oz/¼ cup) olive oil, plus extra if needed

## FOR THE BEEF

2 whole petite tender steaks, 300–400 g (10–14 oz) each
kosher salt
cooking oil spray

### KNOW YOUR CUTS

The petite tender (or teres major in anatomical terms) comes from the chuck or shoulder area of the steer. It has several other aliases: mock or shoulder tender and bistro filet. It's not to be confused with the chuck tender, which is the underblade or supraspinatus muscle.

# PARISA (TEXAS TARTARE)

## SERVES 4-6

Parisa is found only in Medina county in Texas, where locals trace their roots back to the Alsace region of France. I was first introduced to it on a hunting trip near the town of Castroville, and enjoyed it straight out of the butcher's paper with some salty crackers.

## INGREDIENTS

450 g (1 lb) lean beef muscle (see Tip)
1 small white onion
1 jalapeño or serrano chilli
100 g (3½ oz/1 cup) grated
    cheddar cheese
juice of 1 large lime
2 teaspoons garlic powder
1 teaspoon paprika
kosher salt and freshly ground black
    pepper
crackers, for serving

## METHOD

Using a very sharp knife, dice the beef into small chunks—small enough to have several cubes per forkful, but large enough to retain texture. I prefer this chunkier texture, but for a more authentic version you can pass all the ingredients through a grinder to combine them, instead of hand chopping. Place the beef in a bowl.

Finely dice the onion and add to the bowl. Cut the chilli in half and remove the seeds and membrane. Finely dice the chilli and add to the bowl.

Add the cheese, lime juice, garlic powder and paprika and mix with a wooden spoon to combine well. Add salt and pepper a little at a time, tasting and adding more until you reach the desired amount. Serve with crackers and eat immediately.

## KNOW YOUR CUTS

Any tartare requires lean meat for best results. Eye of round is a great choice, but you can also find eye fillet tails (the thin tapering part of the tenderloin muscle) at some butchers. It's an inexpensive but luxurious cut perfect for tartare. Most importantly, whichever cut you use, it's imperative you use extremely fresh beef.

# THE PERFECT STEAK

**SERVES 2 (GENEROUSLY)**

I like to imagine a Stetson-crowned cowboy out under the West Texas stars, grilling this colossal steak over glowing mesquite coals. Steaks cut this thick were built for the reverse sear method (page 27), so you can keep them beautifully pink on the inside while still having a fabulous crusty exterior. Two of these steaks can feed up to four people. For maximum impact, bring them to the table whole, then slice and serve.

## METHOD

Set up a rack on a tray or large plate (to catch drips). Season the rib eyes well on both sides with salt—you should be using at least 1–2 teaspoons per steak. Put the steaks on the rack and place in the fridge, uncovered, at least overnight or up to 36 hours.

Set up a grill for two-zone cooking and heat to medium.

Remove the steaks from the fridge. They should be very dry on the outside, but if there is any remaining moisture, pat dry with paper towel. Do not add any more salt.

Put the steaks over the indirect side of the grill, as far from the heat source as possible, and close the cover. Flip the steaks every 5 minutes, until they reach an internal temperature of 41°C (105°F). Remove from the grill, cover tightly with foil and rest on a tray.

In the meantime, light another half chimney of coals to ensure your fire is raring hot, and add them to the heated coals. At this stage, you may want to consider using specialty anodised aluminium slabs or grates (such as grill grates), which are designed to get 90°C+ (200°F+) hotter than the surface of your grill. If you are using such a tool, place it over the freshly added coals and allow to heat for 10–15 minutes.

It's important that the grill is as hot as you can get it for this final stage; it should be hot enough that you can only bear to hover your hand over the heat for 2–3 seconds. Place the steaks directly over the hot coals and sear for 60–90 seconds, then turn them over and sear for a further 60–90 seconds. Finally, place the narrow side of the steak with the fat cap over the coals to render and blister for a minute. If you still haven't achieved the char you are after, you can flirt with another 30 seconds per side.

The steak is now ready to slice and serve. Sprinkle with sea salt flakes and serve topped with a knob of butter.

## INGREDIENTS

2 cowboy-cut fresh rib eye steaks, 1–1.5 kg (about 2–3 lb) each
kosher salt
sea salt flakes and butter, to serve

### KNOW YOUR CUTS
Cowboy, tomahawk and rib eye steaks are all the same cut, just with differing lengths of bone. The cowboy steak is quite thick, usually at least 4 cm (1½ inches), so has all the wow factor of the tomahawk, but is easier to handle.

147
BEEF

# TWICE-COOKED COLA SHORT RIBS

SERVES 6

Beef short ribs are one of my favourites. They take some cooking to make them tender, but once you've committed to the process, you'll enjoy the results. These ribs are browned then braised in a bath of cola until they yield and soften, then are finished in a super hot oven to crisp up the very outer edges.

## METHOD

Preheat the oven to 160°C (320°F). Season the short ribs well on all sides with salt.

Heat a large pot over high heat, then add the olive oil to the pot. Working in batches, brown the short ribs, taking time to develop a good brown colour. Remove and set aside.

Add the onion, celery and carrots to the pot, then reduce the heat to medium. Cook for 5 minutes so the vegetables can soften slightly, loosening and scraping the browned bits off the bottom of the pot as you stir.

Add the vinegar, Worcestershire sauce, cola, thyme sprigs and bay leaves and cook until the liquid has reduced by half.

Once reduced, add the stock and bring to the boil. Return the ribs to the pot in a single layer, then cover with a lid and transfer to the oven. Cook for 2–3 hours, until the meat is tender and can be pierced with a knife without any resistance. The cooking time will largely depend on the size of your ribs and pot, so start checking that the meat is tender after 2 hours.

Remove the pot from the oven and increase the oven temperature to 220°C (425°F).

Line a baking tray with baking paper. Using kitchen tongs, carefully remove the ribs from the pot and place on the tray, making sure there are no vegetables stuck to the surface of the meat. Place the tray in the hot oven and brown for 10 minutes to create a dark and crusty exterior.

## INGREDIENTS

2 kg (about 4½ lb) bone-in beef short ribs

1–2 tablespoons kosher salt

60 ml (2 fl oz/¼ cup) olive oil

1 large onion, roughly chopped

3 celery stalks, roughly chopped

2 large carrots, roughly chopped

125 ml (4 fl oz/½ cup) balsamic vinegar

60 ml (2 fl oz/¼ cup) Worcestershire sauce

750 ml (26 fl oz/3 cups) cola

6 thyme sprigs

2 bay leaves

750 ml (26 fl oz/3 cups) beef stock (page 205)

### MASTER THE MEAT: BROWNING

This step is important and needs to be done properly because it determines the entire depth of flavour of the finished dish. Patience is key, so make sure to leave the ribs for 10–15 minutes per side, so that a deep colour can develop and form a delicious brown crust.

# CHICKEN FRIED STEAK

## SERVES 4

Brace yourselves: 'chicken fried' actually has nothing to do with chicken! It's actually the style in which the steak is cooked, and it rivals brisket and chili for the most iconic state dish in Texas. Essentially, it's the Lone Star version of schnitzel, but with a fried chicken-style batter instead of breading.

## INGREDIENTS

4 thin round steaks (about 1 kg/2 lb in total)
kosher salt
300 g (10½ oz/2 cups) plain (all-purpose) flour
1 egg
250 ml (9 fl oz/1 cup) milk
2 teaspoons onion powder
2 teaspoons garlic powder
2 teaspoons paprika
1 teaspoon cayenne pepper
1 teaspoon freshly ground black pepper
1.5 litres (52 fl oz/6 cups) vegetable or peanut oil, for deep-frying

## CREAM GRAVY

3 tablespoons bacon fat or butter
35 g (1¼ oz/¼ cup) plain (all-purpose) flour
250-500 ml (9-17 fl oz/1-2 cups) milk
1 tablespoon freshly ground black pepper

### MASTER THE MEAT

CFS traditionally uses the tougher cuts from the hindquarter that need tenderising. To save yourself a little manual labour, ask your butcher to tenderise the steak (two or three times over) for you.

## METHOD

Use the studded side of a meat tenderiser to pound the steaks to a 5 mm (¼ inch) thickness. Season the steaks on both sides with salt.

Coat the steaks in a thin layer of flour and place on a large rack. Combine the egg and 125 ml (4½ fl oz/½ cup) of the milk in a large shallow dish. Put the remaining flour in a large shallow dish and add the onion and garlic powders, paprika, cayenne pepper, 2 teaspoons salt and the black pepper. Whisk with a fork to spread the spices evenly. Add the remaining milk, a little at a time, so the flour mix is damp with some clumps.

Working with one steak at a time, dip it in the egg mix, then immediately place into the damp flour, pressing the flour into the surface to create lots of crust. Return the steaks to the rack to set.

Preheat the oven to 100°C (200°F), or a low warming temperature. Pour the oil into a deep saucepan or deep-fryer and heat to 190°C (375°F). Once the oil has reached the correct temperature, gently place one of the steaks in the hot oil and fry for 2-3 minutes on each side. When golden brown, transfer to another rack and place in the oven to keep warm while you fry the remaining steaks, placing each one in the oven before starting the next. Allow the oil to come up to temperature between cooking each steak.

Once all the steaks are cooked and warming in the oven, you can start the cream gravy. Melt the fat or butter in a frying pan over medium heat. Add the flour and whisk to combine, then toast the roux for 1-2 minutes to cook out the raw flour flavour. Slowly whisk in the milk, a little at a time, until you reach the desired thickness. Add the pepper and season with salt, to taste.

Ladle a generous amount of cream gravy over each steak and serve immediately.

# RICE AND GRAVY

## SERVES 8-10

Sometimes simple names belie truly great dishes, as is the case with Rice and Gravy. The 'gravy' is actually a thick beef stew using braising cuts such as chuck or round. This recipe was taught to me by Ms Linda Armentor, a third generation Cajun from Crowley, Louisiana.

## METHOD

Pat the meat dry with paper towel. Combine the Cajun seasoning, garlic powder, cayenne pepper, salt and pepper in a bowl, then sprinkle over the meat to season well.

Heat the olive oil in a large pot, then add the meat and brown over high heat, working in batches to avoid overcrowding. It's important to get good colour at this stage, as the level of browning will determine the final colour of the gravy. Once the meat is browned, remove and set aside. The pot should have lots of crusty bits stuck on the bottom, which will all help flavour the gravy.

Now add the 'trinity'—the onion, capsicums and celery—and the garlic and cook for about 7 minutes, stirring frequently, until the onion is translucent.

Pour in the stock and stir to combine. Return the meat to the pot and bring to a rolling boil. Reduce the heat to low, cover the pot and simmer for 2½-3 hours, until the meat is tender and falls apart with little resistance. Break up the chunks of meat with a wooden spoon, then stir in the roux to thicken and darken the gravy.

To serve, place a cup of cooked rice in each bowl and ladle the 'gravy' over the top. If you like, serve with a few generous dashes of Home-made hot sauce (page 202).

## INGREDIENTS

1 kg (about 2 lb) beef chuck, cut into large chunks
2 teaspoons Cajun seasoning (page 209)
1 teaspoon garlic powder
½ teaspoon cayenne pepper
1 tablespoon kosher salt
2 teaspoons freshly ground black pepper
60 ml (2 fl oz/¼ cup) olive oil
1 onion, diced
1 green capsicum (bell pepper), diced
1 red capsicum (bell pepper), diced
2 celery stalks, diced
1 garlic clove, crushed
1 litre (35 fl oz/4 cups) beef stock (page 205)
4 tablespoons dark roux (see Tip)
cooked white rice, to serve

### HOW TO MAKE A ROUX

A traditional Cajun roux is made using oil rather than butter. Equal parts of oil and flour are combined in a skillet and slowly stirred over low heat until it transforms to a dark 'mud'. This process can take up to 1 hour and shouldn't be rushed. The darker a roux gets, the less ability it has to thicken, but the richer the flavour. For a single batch of roux, I use 1 cup of flour to 1 cup of oil.

# THE STEAKHOUSE BURGER

## SERVES 4

Do you believe that a real burger should have a mighty meat patty, structurally solid bun and a variety of indulgent toppings? Then this is the burger for you. I call it the Steakhouse burger, and this one is crowned with blue cheese and onion jam.

## INGREDIENTS

750 g (about 1½ lb) minced (ground) chuck or short rib (not lean)

kosher salt

4 burger buns, halved

6–8 tablespoons Onion jam (page 194)

120 g (4¼ oz/1 cup) crumbled blue cheese

## METHOD

Set up a grill for two-zone cooking and heat to high.

Divide the beef into four even portions. Working quickly (so the fat doesn't melt from the heat of your hands), form each portion into a ball, then start to flatten it by tossing it between your hands. Do not overwork the meat or compress it too tightly. Once formed, use your thumb to press a small dent into the top of each burger so it is slightly concave. This keeps the burger even and prevents it puffing on one side during cooking.

Sprinkle each beef patty generously with salt to season well, then place onto the direct heat part of the grill. Sear for 3–4 minutes on each side, until a crust has formed. Once crusted on both sides, move to the indirect side and continue to cook until the meat reaches an internal temperature of 57°C (135°F). This will result in a burger that is pink and juicy in the middle, although not technically cooked to a safe temperature (to read more about safe temperatures and pink burgers, head back to page 16).

Cut the hamburger buns in half, place them over the direct heat, cut side down, and toast for 1–2 minutes.

To assemble the burgers, place a thick patty on the bun base, add a heaped tablespoon of onion jam and sprinkle over the crumbled blue cheese. Finally, nestle the top half of the bun in place to form your steakhouse burger.

## KNOW YOUR CUTS

When referring to minced (ground) beef for burgers, the fat content is usually specified. So 80/20 means 80 per cent muscle with a 20 per cent fat content. Lean beef usually has less than 10 per cent fat, but for the tastiest, juiciest burgers, look for at least 20 and even up to 25 per cent fat.

# THE DOUBLE SMASHBURGER

### SERVES 5

**If you're a fan of fast food-style burgers, with thin patties and simple ingredients, this is the burger for you. Purists insist a great smashburger should have nothing more than meat and cheese in between the buns, but I don't mind a little ketchup and mustard for good measure.**

## METHOD

Preheat a grill or stovetop to high, placing a flat griddle on top to heat up.

Thinly slice the onion and put in a bowl with ¼ teaspoon salt. Divide the beef into 10 portions, then roll each into a ball.

Spray the griddle with a little oil, and place the onions at one end to cook. Keep an eye on the onions as they cook, moving them around with a metal spatula to ensure they soften and brown, but do not burn.

Place the meatballs on the remaining griddle space, allowing enough room to flip the burgers once compressed. If necessary, work in batches to avoid overcrowding.

Using the metal spatula, slowly but firmly 'smash' each ball down to a patty about 1 cm (½ inch) thick. You may need to press them a second time to reach the desired thickness. Season each patty with salt and cook for 2-3 minutes, then flip them over and cook for a further 2 minutes, until a deep brown crust has formed. Layer each patty with cheese and cook for another minute, allowing the cheese to melt.

Cut the hamburger buns in half. Stack the patties onto the bun bases, allowing two patties per burger. Place a generous mound of cooked onions on the patties, then top with ketchup and mustard, if desired. Place the bun top on the stack to finish your burgers.

## INGREDIENTS

1 large white onion

¼ teaspoon kosher salt, plus extra for burger seasoning

1 kg (about 2 lb) minced (ground) chuck or short rib (not lean)

cooking oil spray

10 slices American cheese

5 soft hamburger buns, preferably potato rolls

ketchup and mustard, to serve (optional)

### MASTER THE MEAT
To nail these burgers you're going to need some essential pieces of equipment: a flat griddle (a large, flat cast-iron piece that can go on the stove or grill) and a very firm metal spatula to smash and flip the burgers.

# PATTY MELT PRETZEL BUNS

### MAKES 12-14

The patty melt is a nostalgic American favourite. Simply, it's a double cheeseburger in sandwich form, piled high with caramelised onions and traditionally served on rye bread. I reinterpreted these classic flavours into a soft pretzel bun, which is pulled open to reveal a stuffing of meaty, cheesy goodness.

## PRETZEL DOUGH

250 ml (9 fl oz/1 cup) milk
125 ml (4 fl oz/½ cup) water
2 tablespoons honey
45 g (1½ oz/¼ cup, lightly packed) light brown sugar
2 teaspoons instant dry yeast
450 g (1 lb/3 cups) plain (all-purpose) flour
150 g (5½ oz/1 cup) bread (strong) flour
60 ml (2 fl oz/¼ cup) melted butter
110 g (3¾ oz/½ cup) bicarbonate of soda (baking soda)

## FILLING

2 tablespoons olive oil
400 g (14 oz) minced (ground) beef
1 onion, diced
60 ml (2 fl oz/¼ cup) ketchup
2 tablespoons balsamic vinegar
2 tablespoons Worcestershire sauce
1 tablespoon dijon mustard
1 tablespoon honey
2 teaspoons freshly ground black pepper
kosher salt
310 g (11 oz/2½ cups) grated mozzarella cheese

## METHOD

To make the pretzel dough, combine the milk, water, honey and brown sugar in a microwave-safe bowl. Microwave on high for 30 seconds, then pour the mixture into the bowl of an electric stand mixer. Sprinkle in the yeast and set it aside to bloom for 10-15 minutes.

Add both flours and the melted butter to the yeast mixture. Using the dough hook attachment, mix for 5-7 minutes, until the dough comes together in a large ball.

Place the dough on a floured board or silicone mat. Divide the dough into 12-14 even pieces, rolling each piece into a ball shape. Cover with a damp cloth and allow to proof for 15 minutes.

Using a rolling pin, roll out each ball into a disc about 15 cm (6 inches) in diameter and spread in a single layer on a floured work surface or large mat. Cover again with a damp cloth and leave to proof for 30 minutes.

Meanwhile, to make the filling, heat half the olive oil in a frying pan over medium heat. Add the beef and brown in batches, stirring with a wooden spoon to break up the lumps. Remove from the pan and set aside.

Heat the remaining oil in the pan and brown the onion, then return the meat to the pan. Add the ketchup, balsamic vinegar, Worcestershire sauce, mustard, honey, pepper and season with salt, to taste. Cook for 10-15 minutes, until the liquid reduces and thickens.

Preheat the oven to 220°C (425°F). Line a large baking tray with baking paper. Place a large saucepan of water on the stove to boil.

After the final proof on the dough has completed, put one disc on a board, spoon a tablespoon of the beef mixture into the middle of the disc, then top with a generous spoonful of mozzarella. Gather the sides of the disc at the top and pinch them together, making sure they are sealed well. Place the formed bun on the tray and cover with another damp cloth.

Repeat the process until all the buns have been created. If the unfilled dough discs seem to be getting dry, spritz them with a light mist of water.

Making sure the saucepan of water is at a rolling boil, tip in the bicarbonate of soda, then drop three or four buns in the water. Cook for 15 seconds per side, turning with a mesh strainer or spatula. Make sure you cook only a few buns at a time, to avoid overcrowding the pan. Once boiled, remove the buns using a mesh strainer and return to the tray. Repeat until all the buns have been boiled, then transfer the tray to the oven and cook for 15–20 minutes, until the buns are a dark brown colour. Serve while warm.

PATTY MELT PRETZEL BUNS / PAGE 158

# BEEF HAND PIES

**My cooking style is sort of a mash-up between my native Australia and my adopted home of Texas. This recipe is the perfect example of that fusion, mixing the Southern hand pie (similar to a turnover) with a classic Aussie meat pie, all wrapped up in a flaky pastry shell (similar to an empanada).**

## METHOD

To make the dough, put the flour, sugar and salt in a food processor and pulse to combine. Add the shortening and butter and pulse until the mixture resembles wet sand. Sprinkle the vinegar and 60 ml (2 fl oz/¼ cup) water over the mixture, then pulse to bring the mix together. Add more water, 1 tablespoon at a time, until the dough comes together into a ball. You may not need to use all the extra water.

Turn the dough out onto a lightly floured board, shape into a disc 1–2 cm (½–¾ inch) thick, cover tightly with plastic wrap and place in the fridge for at least 2 hours or overnight.

To make the filling, heat the oil in a large saucepan over high heat. Brown the beef in batches, seasoning well with salt as it cooks. Use a slotted spoon to remove the beef to a bowl, leaving the oil and fat in the pan. Add the onion to the pan and cook for 7 minutes, or until softened. Return the beef to the pan, then stir in the Worcestershire sauce, barbecue sauce, ketchup, Vegemite (if using) and pepper.

Put the cornflour in a small bowl, add 1 tablespoon of the stock and stir to make a paste. Add this to the beef, then add the remaining stock. Reduce the heat to low and simmer for about 20 minutes, or until the mix has thickened and most of the liquid has reduced. Set aside to cool before using.

Preheat the oven to 220°C (425°F). Line a large baking tray with baking paper.

Divide the dough disc into eight portions. Working with one portion at a time, roll out the dough into a flat disc no more than 5 mm (¼ inch) thick. Scoop about half a cup of cooled beef mixture, draining any excess liquid, and place in the centre of the disc. Fold one side of the disc over to meet the other, forming a half moon. Crimp the edges to seal, then place on the tray. Repeat until all pies have been formed. Using a pastry brush, brush the egg over the tops of the pies. Transfer to the oven and bake for 20–30 minutes until golden brown.

## DOUGH

335 g (11¾ oz/2¼ cups) plain (all-purpose) flour
2 teaspoons sugar
½ teaspoon kosher salt
65 g (2¼ oz) vegetable shortening
125 g (4½ oz) chilled butter, diced
2 tablespoons apple cider vinegar
60 ml (2 fl oz/¼ cup) ice water, plus 4 tablespoons

## FILLING

2 tablespoons vegetable or olive oil
500 g (about 1 lb) minced (ground) beef
2 teaspoons kosher salt
1 onion, finely diced
2 tablespoons Worcestershire sauce
60 ml (2 fl oz/¼ cup) barbecue sauce
2 tablespoons ketchup
2 teaspoons Vegemite (optional)
2 teaspoons freshly ground black pepper
1 tablespoon cornflour (cornstarch)
125 ml (4 fl oz/½ cup) beef stock (page 205)
1 egg, lightly whisked

# CHILLI-CRUSTED ROAST BEEF

## SERVES 6-8

Roast beef is unbelievably easy to master—it's a classic dish for a cold winter's evening that yields lots of leftovers for piling high onto sandwiches the next day. Herbed crusts are common for beef, but the flavour and subtle heat of the roasted chillies is something special!

### INGREDIENTS

1.3–1.5 kg (about 3 lb) roast beef, such as chuck or topside
80 g (2¾ oz/⅓ cup) American (yellow) mustard
1 tablespoon wholegrain mustard
2 tablespoons Worcestershire sauce
2 teaspoons paprika
2 teaspoons onion powder
3 teaspoons coarsely ground black pepper
3–4 fresh green chillies, diced
kosher salt

### METHOD

Preheat the oven to 190°C (375°F). Set up a wire rack in a roasting pan. Prepare the roast beef by cutting away any large fat caps or sinew, although most butchers will have already done this for you.

Put both mustards in a bowl, along with the Worcestershire sauce, paprika, onion powder, pepper and chillies. Stir to combine until a chunky paste is created.

Season the beef generously with salt, then put the roast on the rack. Press the paste all over the top and sides of the meat to form a crust about 5 mm (¼ inch) thick all over. It's easiest to do this using clean hands, but you can use a spatula if you prefer.

Place the beef in the oven and cook for 50–60 minutes, until the internal temperature reaches 60°C (140°F). Transfer to a board, cover loosely with foil and rest for at least 20 minutes before carving and serving.

# SMOKED BEEF CHEEKS

## SERVES 4-6

Brisket is arguably the king of all barbecued meats, and as more people get into low 'n' slow cooking it's often the first thing they want to try. But brisket is also one of the hardest things to smoke to perfection and can take up to 16 hours to cook. The solution? Beef cheeks. These little marvels are just like baby briskets, but take just 5 hours to transform into barbecue bounty. Turn them into simple barbacoa tacos by piling the meat into a tortilla and drizzling with Jalapeño 'crack' sauce (page 203).

## METHOD

Prepare a smoker to cook at 135°C (275°F), a little hotter than traditional low and slow. I recommend using a neutral wood such as North American post oak or Australian ironbark.

Rub the cheeks generously with the brisket rub and then the Hardcore Carnivore meat seasoning (if using), making sure every side is covered and pressing the rub into the meat. Hardcore Carnivore: Black is my own rub, and has activated charcoal in it, so it will help create a lovely dark bark.

Place the beef cheeks in the smoker. To keep an eye on the temperature as you cook, you may choose to use a probe monitor, but also check the temperature every few hours with a hand-held thermometer.

Smoke until the cheeks reach an internal temperature of 99°C (210°F), which will take about 5 hours. Remove, cover with butcher's paper or foil and rest for 30 minutes, then slice or pull the beef cheeks to serve.

## INGREDIENTS

4-5 denuded beef cheeks (see Tip)
375 g (13 oz/1½ cups) Basic brisket rub (page 206)
50 g (1¾ oz/¼ cup) Hardcore Carnivore: Black meat seasoning (optional)

### KNOW YOUR CUTS

Just like brisket, beef cheeks are rippled with collagen, which converts to gelatine during the cooking process, making the finished product rich and sumptuous. Ordering the cheeks 'denuded' means they will come trimmed of any membrane or silver skin and be ready to go.

# CHAPTER SIX

SIDES

# TEXAS CAVIAR

**SERVES 6-8**

The name may be somewhat misleading, as the 'caviar' in this dish is actually black-eyed peas. There have been many variations of this salad over the years, with people adding ingredients such as corn, tomato or coriander (cilantro) to make their own signature version. Serve this fresh, zesty salad as a dip with tortilla chips or as a side dish for summer barbecues.

## INGREDIENTS

400 g (14 oz) can black beans, rinsed and drained

400 g (14 oz) can black-eyed peas, rinsed and drained

1 red capsicum (bell pepper), seeded and diced

1 small red onion, diced

1 jalapeño chilli, seeded and finely diced

1 teaspoon chopped oregano

3-4 spring onions (scallions), chopped

1 garlic clove, crushed

125 ml (4 fl oz/½ cup) vegetable oil

60 ml (2 fl oz/¼ cup) red wine vinegar

1 teaspoon Worcestershire sauce

kosher salt and freshly ground black pepper

## METHOD

Put the beans, peas, capsicum, onion, jalapeño, oregano and spring onions in a bowl. Add the garlic, vegetable oil, vinegar and Worcestershire sauce. Season well with salt and pepper.

Cover the bowl with plastic wrap and place in the fridge to marinate for 4-6 hours. Drain off the excess liquid and serve cold.

# FENNEL, PEAR AND WALNUT SALAD

**SERVES 6**

**Fresh acidic sides tend to match well with game meats, serving as an antidote to the richness and cutting through the fat. I like to serve this with my Pan-seared duck breasts (page 70).**

## METHOD

Chop off the very end of the fennel bulb, then use a knife or mandolin to thinly slice the fennel until you start reaching the green parts at the top. Place the sliced fennel in a bowl.

Roughly chop a few of the feathery fronds from the top of the fennel and add to the bowl. Discard the remainder of the fennel.

Cut the pear in quarters lengthways, then cut away the tough core from each quarter, discarding the stem. Slice each quarter thinly and add to the bowl. Add the walnuts to the fennel and pear.

Put the olive oil, vinegar, lemon juice, agave and pepper in a small jar. Seal with the lid and shake vigorously to combine. Pour the dressing over the salad, then toss a few times with your hands to ensure everything is well coated.

## INGREDIENTS

1 fennel bulb
1 corella pear
2 tablespoons roughly chopped walnuts
2 tablespoons olive oil
1 tablespoon white wine vinegar
2 teaspoons lemon juice
2 teaspoons agave nectar
½ teaspoon freshly ground black pepper

### SWAP IT OUT

The agave has a delicate, neutral flavour that adds a subtle sweetness, but you can swap it out with honey.

# TANGY VINEGAR SLAW

## SERVES 6-8

This fresh coleslaw has very little mayo and a little kick of spice from the chipotle powder. The tangy apple cider vinegar makes it a perfect pairing with pork. It's best made and served the same day for maximum crunch and to avoid the dreaded soggy slaw.

### INGREDIENTS

½ green cabbage
¼ red cabbage (optional, for colour variation)
1 large carrot
25 g (1 oz/½ cup) chopped coriander (cilantro) leaves
120 g (4¼ oz/½ cup) mayonnaise
125 ml (4 fl oz/½ cup) buttermilk
80 ml (2½ fl oz/⅓ cup) apple cider vinegar
1 tablespoon sugar
1 teaspoon freshly ground black pepper
½ teaspoon chipotle powder
kosher salt

### METHOD

Thinly slice the green and red cabbages, taking care to cut out and discard the thick core. Place in a large bowl. Coarsely grate the carrot on a box grater, then add to the cabbage, along with the chopped coriander.

In a small bowl, combine the mayonnaise, buttermilk, vinegar, sugar, pepper and chipotle powder. Whisk to combine, then taste and add salt as needed.

Pour the dressing over the cabbage mix and stir to combine well. Place in the fridge for at least 1 hour before serving, to allow the flavours to mellow and mingle.

# SMOKED GARLIC POTATO SALAD

## SERVES 6-8

I usually serve this salad when barbecue is on the menu, since the smoker is already fired up. Consider doubling the recipe to give yourself some leftovers for the next day; it's even better once the flavours have had a chance to mingle together.

## METHOD

Start by smoking the garlic. Cut the tops off the garlic bulbs to expose the cloves inside. Place them in a microwave-safe container with 2 tablespoons water at the bottom (to create steam). Cover and microwave on medium power for 5-6 minutes to par-cook.

Preheat a charcoal grill to medium or fire up a smoker to 120°C (250°F). Create a shallow 'boat' of foil and place the garlic bulbs inside. If using a smoker, place the garlic in the smoker for 20-25 minutes, until the cloves are completely soft. If using a charcoal grill, throw a generous handful of wood chips onto the coals, then place the foil boat with the garlic on the grill. Close the lid and cook for 20-25 minutes, until the garlic is completely soft. Allow to cool.

Place the whole potatoes in a large saucepan of cold water and bring to the boil. Boil for 15-20 minutes, until the potatoes are just tender—you should be able to pierce them with a knife with no resistance. Drain immediately.

Squeeze the garlic cloves out from the papery skin into a food processor or blender. Pulse several times until smooth. Add the mayonnaise, sour cream, lemon juice and vinegar and pulse again to combine. Stir in the mustard and parsley.

Transfer the mayonnaise to a large bowl. Cut the cooled potatoes into chunks, then add to the bowl and toss to coat with the dressing. Season to taste with salt and pepper.

## INGREDIENTS

3 whole garlic bulbs
2 kg (about 4½ lb) red potatoes, washed and skin on
120 g (4¼ oz/½ cup) mayonnaise
65 g (2¼ oz/¼ cup) sour cream
2 tablespoons lemon juice
2 tablespoons apple cider vinegar
1 tablespoon wholegrain mustard
2 tablespoons chopped flat-leaf (Italian) parsley
kosher salt and freshly ground black pepper

# BEER-BATTERED ONION RINGS

**SERVES 6-8**

The golden crust on each ring is heavenly—it's light and airy with a phenomenal crunch. These onion rings are right at home piled impossibly high next to a steak. The trick to ensuring they are crisp and light without being greasy is all about the temperature of the oil (check the guide on page 15).

## INGREDIENTS

4 large onions

300 g (10½ oz/2 cups) plain (all-purpose) flour

1–1.5 litres (35–52 fl oz/4–6 cups) oil, for deep-frying (peanut oil is best but vegetable works great too)

125 g (4½ oz/1 cup) cornflour (cornstarch)

1½ teaspoons onion powder

1½ teaspoons garlic powder

1½ teaspoons chipotle powder

1 teaspoon cayenne pepper

2 teaspoons sugar

1 tablespoon kosher salt

350 ml (12 fl oz) good-quality beer (use a lager or pilsner)

250 ml (9 fl oz/1 cup) soda water or mineral water

1 egg, lightly whisked

## METHOD

Peel and then slice the onions into rings 1–2 cm (½–¾ inch) wide. You will only be able to use the larger middle to outer rings for this, so chop up the centre pieces and store them in the freezer for your next recipe.

Toss the rings in 75 g (2¾ oz/½ cup) of the flour and set aside. Set up a cooling rack and layer with some paper towel.

Pour the oil into a heavy-based saucepan (or deep-fryer if you have one) and heat until the temperature registers between 180°C and 190°C (350°F and 375°F).

In a large bowl, combine the remaining flour, cornflour, onion, garlic and chipotle powders, cayenne pepper, sugar and salt.

Once your oil is at the correct temperature, add the beer, soda water and egg to the dry ingredients in the bowl and work quickly to whisk the mixture together.

Dip each onion ring into the batter, remove and allow a few seconds for most of the batter to drip off before placing into the oil. You can use your hands (with care) to place the onion rings into the oil, or use tongs if you prefer. Repeat with a few more rings, making sure you don't overcrowd the pan. Fry the onion rings, turning them now and then, until golden, then remove and place on the paper towel to drain.

Transfer the drained onion rings to a baking tray lined with baking paper and keep warm in a low (120°C/250°F) oven until all the batches are cooked. Repeat with the next batch, letting the temperature of the oil come back up to 180°C (350°F) between batches.

# GIANT ONE-PAN HASHBROWN

## SERVES 4-6

My grandmother used to make this carbolicious dish every week, the potato shreds flecked with a generous amount of black pepper. It's sort of a hybrid between a latke, hashbrown and Spanish tortilla. Pair this with the petite tender (page 143) for a fancier take on steak 'n' taters.

### INGREDIENTS
2 large or 3 medium potatoes, peeled
4 saltine or water crackers
1 egg
2 teaspoons kosher salt
1 teaspoon freshly ground black pepper
2-3 tablespoons olive oil

### METHOD
Grate the potatoes on the side of the grater with larger holes, then place in a bowl. Use your hands to squeeze out the extra moisture from the grated potato. Discard the liquid.

Place the crackers in a resealable plastic bag and bash with a rolling pin or meat tenderiser until they resemble fine crumbs. Add the crumbs to the bowl, along with the egg, salt and pepper. Stir to combine well.

Heat a large frying pan over high heat and add the olive oil. Once the oil has heated for 1-2 minutes, pour in the potato mix. Cook for 4-6 minutes, then reduce the heat to medium and cook for a further 5-10 minutes, until the edges have turned crispy and the mix starts to change colour and appears firmer.

Use a spatula to gently lift the hashbrown and check that the base is browned. Once it is, place a plate over the pan, then carefully but quickly flip the pan and plate so the hashbrown is on the plate. Slide it back into the pan, cooked side up. Increase the heat slightly and cook until the bottom side is golden.

Slide the hashbrown onto a plate, cut into wedges and serve while hot and crisp.

# FOUR-CHEESE MAC AND CHEESE

## SERVES 6-8

Although technically a side dish, a big bowl of this uber-cheesy pasta is absolutely a meal in itself. For an instant carnivore's version, stir through some left-over shredded lamb (page 128), some pulled pork (page 95) or smoked beef cheeks (page 167).

I can't give a scientific reason why, but I always use shell pasta for mac 'n' cheese simply because I think it's tastier. Perhaps it's because the pasta shells are like little cups that hold extra sauce?

## METHOD

Cook the pasta in a saucepan of boiling salted water until just before *al dente*. Because the pasta will be cooked twice, you want it to have some good bite to it at this stage. Drain and set aside.

Preheat the oven to 190°C (375°F). Melt the butter in a large saucepan over medium heat, then whisk in the flour to create a roux. Cook the roux, stirring frequently, for 3-5 minutes to cook out the raw flour taste.

Slowly pour in the milk, whisking to emulsify into a sauce, and getting rid of any lumps, then slowly pour in the wine or beer. Add the four cheeses and stir until melted, then cook for a further 5-7 minutes to thicken slightly.

Stir in the mustard, paprika, sage, nutmeg and salt. Add the cooked pasta and stir into the cheese sauce.

Pour the whole mixture into a large skillet or baking dish, sprinkle the panko over the top and spritz with a spray or two of oil. Transfer to the oven and bake for 30-35 minutes, until golden on top. Allow to cool slightly before serving, as the cheese will be very hot.

## INGREDIENTS

500 g (about 1 lb) uncooked shell pasta
2 tablespoons butter
2 tablespoons plain (all-purpose) flour
250 ml (9 fl oz/1 cup) milk
250 ml (9 fl oz/1 cup) white wine or beer
100 g (3½ oz/1 cup) grated gouda cheese
100 g (3½ oz/1 cup) grated asiago or fontina cheese
100 g (3½ oz/1 cup) grated gruyère cheese
100 g (3½ oz/1 cup) grated cheddar cheese
1 tablespoon dijon mustard
½ teaspoon smoked paprika
¼ teaspoon ground sage
¼ teaspoon ground nutmeg
1 teaspoon kosher salt
30 g (1 oz/½ cup) panko breadcrumbs
cooking oil spray

### SWAP IT OUT
If you can't find asiago or fontina cheese, use colby.

# CHARRED BRUSSELS SPROUTS WITH GUANCIALE

### SERVES 4-6

**These ain't yo mama's sprouts, y'all! Guanciale is cured pork jowl, similar to pancetta. It renders down when you cook it, leaving lots of salty, delicious pork fat to fry up the sprouts. Look for the smaller baby sprouts, which are more tender than their larger counterparts.**

## METHOD

Cut the tough stems off the brussels sprouts if they are large, then split each in half lengthways.

Chop the guanciale into small pieces. Place in a frying pan over medium heat and cook until the fat has rendered and the meat pieces are crispy. Use a slotted spoon to remove the meat to a bowl, leaving the rendered fat in the pan.

Place the brussels sprouts in the pan, cut side down. Leave to cook for 3–4 minutes, until the cut side is browned, then flip them over and cook the other side for a further 3–4 minutes. Season the sprouts with the salt and pepper.

Return the guanciale pieces to the pan and cook for a further 5 minutes, stirring occasionally. Add the vinegar and a little lemon juice, if desired, and cook for a few more minutes, or until the sprouts are just tender. Serve immediately.

## INGREDIENTS

300 g (10½ oz) brussels sprouts
100 g (3½ oz) guanciale
½ teaspoon kosher salt
½ teaspoon freshly ground black pepper
2–3 tablespoons balsamic vinegar
squeeze of lemon (optional)

# CEDAR-PLANKED BRIE WITH FIG WALNUT PASTE

## SERVES 6-8

Cedar planks can be found at specialty barbecue supply retailers. They are placed directly on the grill, creating an incredible perfumed smoke that permeates the cheese, which is served warm and runny. Serve as a snack or appetiser.

## INGREDIENTS

1 cedar grilling plank
200 g (7 oz) dried figs
2 tablespoons lemon juice
185 ml (6 fl oz/¾ cup) water
3 tablespoons light brown sugar
90 g (3¼ oz/¾ cup) chopped walnuts
1 x 200 g (7 oz) wheel of brie

## METHOD

Immerse the cedar plank in water to soak for at least 1 hour.

Cut the hard nub off the end of the figs, then place in a saucepan with the lemon juice and water. Bring to the boil, then reduce the heat to low and simmer for 10–15 minutes, or until the figs have softened. It may help to break up the larger figs with a spoon as they cook.

Remove the pan from the heat and leave to cool a little, then use an immersion or stick blender to blend into a paste.

Return the fig paste to the stove over low heat. Add the brown sugar and walnuts and cook until the mixture thickens, stirring often.

Heat a grill to medium. Remove the plank from the water and pat the surface dry. Place the wheel of brie on top, then put the plank on the grill and close the lid. The bottom of the plank will char and smoke; this is normal and desirable, as long as it's not actually on fire with flames. If you are having trouble keeping it from igniting, move it to a cooler part of the grill.

Cook the brie for 10–12 minutes, until the rind has bronzed and is puffed, checking on it every few minutes to ensure there are no flames.

Spoon generous amounts of the fig walnut paste on top of the brie and serve immediately.

# SAMBAL BOK CHOY

## SERVES 4–6

Sambal should be a staple condiment in everyone's fridge. It's a chilli and garlic paste that can be added to everything from salad dressings to chicken wings. Thrown into a pan with some Asian greens, it quickly creates a simple, spicy side dish.

### INGREDIENTS
4–5 baby bok choy (pak choy)
2 tablespoons vegetable oil
1 cm (½ inch) piece of fresh ginger, grated or very finely diced
1 garlic clove, crushed
2 teaspoons sambal oelek
¼ teaspoon chilli flakes
1 teaspoon sesame oil
kosher salt

### METHOD
Remove any dark outer leaves from the bok choy, then slice in half lengthways.

Place a large wok or frying pan over very high heat and add the vegetable oil. When the oil is hot, add the ginger and garlic and cook for about 30 seconds, stirring constantly, until fragrant. Do not let the ginger and garlic burn, as it will add a bitter taste to the dish.

Add the halved bok choy and sambal oelek to the wok and stir-fry for about 5 minutes, or until the leaves have wilted but the stems are still crisp.

Add the chilli flakes, drizzle with the sesame oil and season with salt, to taste. Remove from the heat and serve.

# GRILLED ROMAINE LETTUCE

**Believe it or not, a quick sear to a wedge of this lettuce (known as cos in Australia) creates some wondrous charred magic. If you don't want to grill it, you can get a similar result by using a cast-iron pan. This is an ideal side dish to pair with any grilled meats, and a convenient pairing since the grill will already be fired up.**

## METHOD

Heat a grill to high.

Remove the dark outer leaves from the lettuces, then cut each lettuce in half lengthways. Brush the cut sides with olive oil and season with salt and pepper.

Place the lettuces on the grill, cut side down, and leave for 3–4 minutes, until they have developed a nice char. Flip them over and cook for a further 4–5 minutes.

Remove from the heat and place on a tray, cut side up. Squeeze some lemon over each half. Finely grate the cheese over the lettuce and serve immediately.

## INGREDIENTS

2 cos (romaine) lettuces

2 tablespoons olive oil

kosher salt and freshly ground black pepper

1 lemon, cut into wedges

75 g (2¾ oz) pecorino romano or parmesan cheese, in a block

GRILLED ROMAINE LETTUCE / PAGE 185

# JALAPEÑO CORNBREAD

The addition of cream corn amps up the corn flavour while helping to keep the bread moist. You can use this base recipe to create other flavour combinations by adding extra ingredients such as cheese or bacon (or both!). Cornbread makes for a wonderful side to smoked meats and roasts. Any leftovers are also delicious for breakfast with a little extra butter and a drizzle of honey.

## METHOD

Preheat the oven to 230°C (450°F). Put the lard or oil in a 30 cm (12 inch) cast-iron skillet or baking dish and place in the warm oven to melt.

Combine all the dry ingredients in a bowl, stirring with a whisk to mix well. Add the egg, corn, jalapeño and buttermilk. Stir until the mixture is just combined—the consistency should be quite thick.

After the pan has been in the oven for at least 10 minutes, remove it and work quickly to transfer the batter to the hot pan. Be careful: the pan and grease will be extremely hot. Reduce the oven temperature to 180°C (350°F) and immediately return the pan to the oven.

Bake for 25-35 minutes, or until a toothpick inserted into the middle comes out clean.

## INGREDIENTS

2 tablespoons pork lard or oil (pork lard tastes MUCH better!)

270 g (9½ oz/2 cups) cornmeal (white or yellow) or fine polenta

75 g (2¾ oz/½ cup) plain (all-purpose) flour

1½ teaspoons baking powder

½ teaspoon bicarbonate of soda (baking soda)

2 teaspoons kosher salt, or to taste

1 tablespoon sugar

1 teaspoon paprika

1 egg

310 g (11 oz) can cream corn

1-2 jalapeño chillies, seeded and finely diced

375 ml (13 fl oz/1½ cups) buttermilk

# FAT-ROASTED POTATOES

## SERVES 4-6

If you were looking for the best roast potatoes, you have found them. You can use a variety of different fats to create these spuds, and they'll always turn out with perfect fluffy interiors and a phenomenal crunch.

### INGREDIENTS
4-5 large roasting potatoes
3-4 tablespoons beef, pork, duck
   or goose fat
kosher salt

### METHOD
Preheat the oven to 230°C (450°F). Peel and then dice the potatoes into large chunks.

Put the potatoes in a large saucepan of salted cold water and bring to the boil. Cook for 7-10 minutes to par-boil the potatoes, or until a sharp knife can pierce them with medium resistance. The key here is to cook them enough that the outsides are soft and will 'fluff up', but not so much that they are cooked all the way through.

While the potatoes are boiling, put the fat in a roasting pan and place the pan in the oven to heat. This step should take no longer than 10 minutes, otherwise the fat will begin to smoke.

Drain the potatoes into a colander, then shake vigorously to rough and fluff the exterior. You can use a metal spoon to toss them around a little, to make the edges really shaggy. The more you do this, the crispier the results.

Carefully pour the potatoes into the pan with the hot, melted fat. Take care, as they will sputter and spit a bit as they hit the fat. Sprinkle with salt and return the pan to the oven to roast for 40-50 minutes, or until evenly golden and crisp. Check on the potatoes two or three times during the cooking time, and toss them around in the pan with a spoon to make sure all sides have contact with the fat.

When the potatoes are cooked, transfer to paper towel to drain (only if there is still some fat left in the bottom of the pan), and serve while still warm.

### HOW TO RENDER FAT
To render your own pork fat or beef tallow, you're going to need large pieces of fat to start. Place them in a large saucepan with a little water over low heat. As the water evaporates, the fat will begin to render down, eventually completely melting into liquid, with any bits of skin or meat turned into crisp nuggets. Allow to cool, then carefully strain to remove any impurities. Store in an airtight jar in the fridge for up to 4 months.

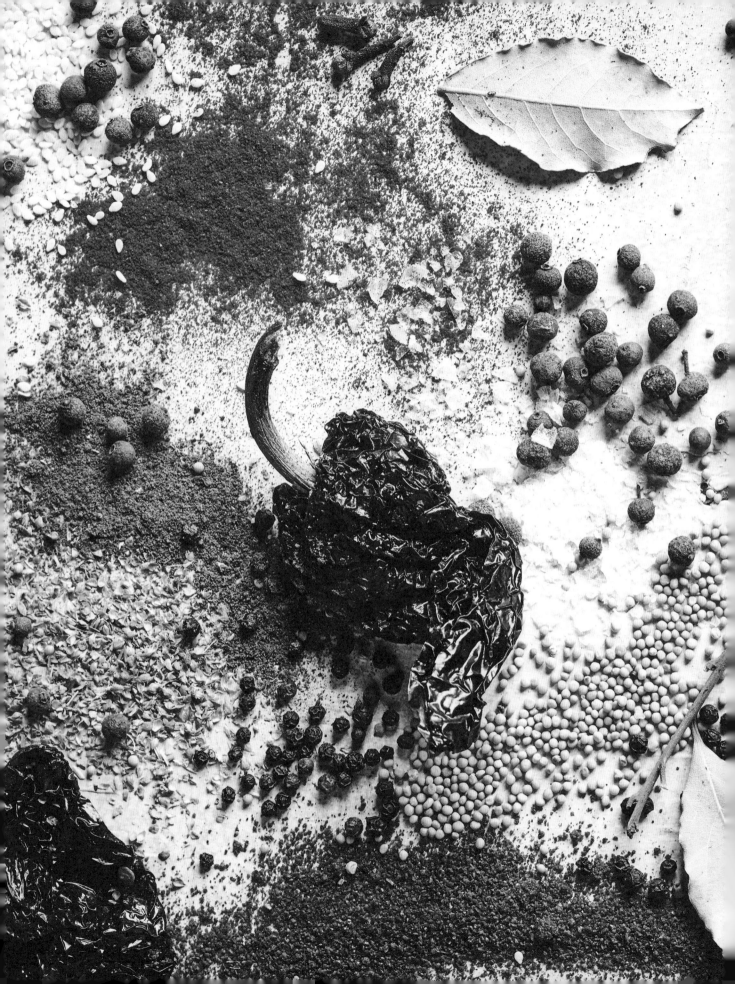

# CHAPTER SEVEN

## FOUNDATIONS AND FINISHES

# CONDIMENTS AND SAUCES

From a regional trio of barbecue sauces to home-made beer mustard, many of these core condiments and sauces may end up being staples in your fridge.

## ONION JAM

### MAKES ABOUT 300 G (10½ OZ/1 CUP)

This onion jam is a feature of my Steakhouse burger (page 154). Pair it with steaks, use it in grilled cheese sandwiches or simply spread it on a cracker and enjoy as is.

### INGREDIENTS

3 large onions, peeled
2 teaspoons olive oil
1 teaspoon chipotle powder
½ teaspoon garlic powder
½ teaspoon kosher salt
60 ml (2 fl oz/¼ cup) balsamic vinegar
90 g (3¼ oz/¼ cup) honey
110 g (3¾ oz/½ cup, firmly packed) light brown sugar
125 ml (4 fl oz/½ cup) water
3 thyme sprigs

### METHOD

Cut each onion in half, then thinly slice each half into thin half-moons.

Place a large saucepan over medium heat. Add the olive oil and onion slices and cook, stirring often, until the onions begin to brown.

Add the chipotle powder, garlic powder, salt, vinegar, honey, brown sugar and water. Stir to combine. Throw in the thyme and simmer over low heat, stirring occasionally, until the mixture thickens and most of the liquid has evaporated. Store in an airtight container in the fridge for up to 1 week.

# HOME-MADE BEER MUSTARD

## MAKES ABOUT 250 G (9 OZ/1 CUP)

Mustard is actually quite easy to make. This mustard has a chunkier finish, but if you prefer a smoother mustard, simply blend it for longer. You can also add a little turmeric to your mustard for a brighter yellow appearance.

### INGREDIENTS
40 g (1½ oz/¼ cup) yellow mustard seeds
40 g (1½ oz/¼ cup) brown mustard seeds
250 ml (9 fl oz/1 cup) beer (I use an amber ale)
1 teaspoon kosher salt
1 tablespoon honey
60 ml (2 fl oz/¼ cup) white wine vinegar

### METHOD
Put the yellow and brown mustard seeds in a bowl and pour in the beer. Cover and place in the fridge to soak overnight.

Add the salt, honey and vinegar and blend lightly with a stick blender until the mix has emulsified, but there are still chunks of whole seeds. Place in an airtight jar and leave in the fridge at least overnight before using. Store in an airtight container in the fridge for up to 1 month.

# TRUFFLED BUTTER

## MAKES ABOUT 130 G (4½ OZ)

Freshly grated truffle is perhaps the ultimate ingredient, but it's an expensive luxury. Truffle pastes or 'zests' are mixed with a few other ingredients to make them more affordable, but will still work perfectly for your butter if you can't use pure truffle. Even more affordable still, you can combine the butter with truffle-scented oil for the most economical version. You can use any kind of salt here, but I prefer the salty bursts the bigger chunks of fleur de sel or sea salt flakes add.

### INGREDIENTS
125 g (4½ oz) butter
fleur de sel or sea salt flakes
freshly grated truffle, truffle paste or oil, to taste

### METHOD
Put the butter in a bowl and leave to soften at room temperature. Sprinkle with salt and your preferred truffle additive and stir well to combine. When you add the truffle, add a little at a time—it's very pungent and a little will go a long way. Season with salt, then scrape the butter onto a piece of plastic wrap, roll into a cylinder and refrigerate until firm.

Cut discs off the truffle butter log as needed, to top steaks, corn and anything else you want to add a little luxury to. Store in the fridge for up to 1 month.

# EASY PINK PEPPERCORN AND RED WINE REDUCTION

## MAKES ABOUT 125 ML (4 FL OZ/½ CUP)

This reduction is a great choice for those who can't choose between red wine or pepper sauce for their steaks. For a more prominent pepper flavour, add a teaspoon of cracked black pepper.

### INGREDIENTS
250 ml (9 fl oz/1 cup) red wine
1 tablespoon pink peppercorns
1 teaspoon kosher salt
2 tablespoons butter, cut into cubes

### METHOD
Put the wine and peppercorns in a saucepan and simmer over low heat until the mixture has reduced to 60 ml (2 fl oz/¼ cup). Add the salt and then whisk in the butter, a few cubes at a time, until the mixture thickens slightly and becomes glossy. Serve while warm.

# CLASSIC BÉARNAISE

## MAKES ABOUT 250 ML (9 FL OZ/1 CUP)

The classic French sauce to accompany steak, béarnaise is a more complex version of hollandaise sauce. It's traditionally made with a double boiler to stop the sauce from splitting, but using a stick blender is a much easier method.

### INGREDIENTS
60 ml (2 fl oz/¼ cup) white wine vinegar
60 ml (2 fl oz/¼ cup) white wine
2 tablespoons chopped tarragon
2 tablespoons finely chopped French shallots
8 whole peppercorns
1 teaspoon kosher salt
2 egg yolks
170 g (6 oz) unsalted butter, melted

### METHOD
Put the vinegar and wine in a saucepan along with 1 tablespoon of the tarragon, the shallots and peppercorns. Place the pan over medium heat and simmer for 5–7 minutes, until the mixture has reduced to a few tablespoons. Strain through a sieve and set aside to cool.

Combine the cooled liquid, salt and egg yolks in a jug and blitz with an immersion or stick blender for a few seconds. Leaving the blender on, slowly add the melted butter in a stream, emulsifying the mixture. Add the remaining tarragon and blend for a few more seconds. Taste for seasoning and add extra salt if needed, then serve immediately.

# HORSERADISH CRÈME FRAÎCHE

I love the pairing of horseradish with beef, but always felt the traditional creams were too thin or aerated. Crème fraîche has a much thicker and creamier consistency, with a gentle hint of sourness and a velvety finish. If you don't want to make your own crème fraîche from scratch, just substitute with store bought and add the horseradish and salt.

## INGREDIENTS
250 ml (9 fl oz/1 cup) thickened (heavy) cream
2 tablespoons cultured buttermilk
2 tablespoons freshly grated or prepared
   horseradish
¼ teaspoon kosher salt

## METHOD
Put the cream in a non-reactive container (a glass jar is best). Add the buttermilk and cover with a cloth (or something that is breathable but keeps anything from flying in to the mix).

Place in a warm part of the kitchen and let it sit for 12–24 hours. Start checking that it's the right consistency after 12 hours; the crème fraîche will continue to thicken, even once refrigerated.

Stir in the horseradish and salt. Store in an airtight container in the fridge for up to 1 week.

# LOUISIANA REMOULADE

MAKES ABOUT 375 ML (13 FL OZ/1½ CUPS)

I've paired this remoulade with the Cajun brick yardbird (page 61), although it makes a great all-purpose dipping sauce in place of ranch dressing.

## INGREDIENTS
230 g (8 oz/1 cup) mayonnaise
1 garlic clove, minced
30 g (1 oz/¼ cup) finely chopped spring onions
   (scallions)
1 tablespoon grated horseradish
2 tablespoons dijon or Creole mustard
1 tablespoon paprika
¼ teaspoon cayenne pepper
3–4 dashes hot sauce (ready-made or see
   page 202)
1 teaspoon Worcestershire sauce
1 tablespoon lemon juice
kosher salt and freshly ground black pepper,
   to taste
60 ml (2 fl oz/¼ cup) olive oil

## METHOD
Put all the ingredients, except the olive oil, in a bowl. Stir to combine well. Drizzle in the olive oil, whisking to combine. Store in an airtight container in the fridge for up to 1 week.

ONION JAM / PAGE 194

CAROLINA MUSTARD SAUCE / PAGE 201

KANSAS CITY-STYLE
BARBECUE SAUCE / PAGE 200

ALABAMA WHITE SAUCE / PAGE 201

# KANSAS CITY-STYLE BARBECUE SAUCE

## MAKES ABOUT 500 ML (17 FL OZ/2 CUPS)

Root beer is not a traditional ingredient in barbecue sauce, but adds extra sweetness and a subtle 'can't tell what it is but it sure tastes good' background flavour. If you prefer your sauce even sweeter, add in half a cup of honey. You'll find root beer from some larger supermarkets and specialty stores and delis.

## INGREDIENTS

500 ml (17 fl oz/2 cups) root beer
1 large onion, roughly chopped into large chunks
2–3 chipotle chillies (canned in adobo sauce)
2 teaspoons crushed garlic
700 ml (24 fl oz) tomato passata (puréed tomatoes)
3 tablespoons Worcestershire sauce
185 ml (6 fl oz/¾ cup) apple cider vinegar
2 tablespoons lemon juice
60 g (2¼ oz/¼ cup) American (yellow) mustard
90 g (3¼ oz/¼ cup) molasses
110 g (3¾ oz/½ cup, firmly packed) light brown sugar
2 tablespoons vegetable oil
kosher salt

## METHOD

Pour the root beer into a small saucepan and simmer over low heat until it reduces down to about 125 ml (4 fl oz/½ cup). The final reduction should be thick and syrupy.

Put the onion, chipotle chillies and garlic in a blender and blend until a smooth paste forms.

Scrape the paste into a large saucepan over medium heat and cook for 4–6 minutes, stirring frequently. Add the passata, Worcestershire sauce, vinegar, lemon juice, mustard and root beer syrup and stir to combine. Add the molasses, brown sugar and vegetable oil, then stir to combine. Season with salt to taste.

Reduce the heat to low and simmer gently for at least 20–30 minutes, until the sauce thickens. Allow to cool and then store in the fridge for up to 1 month.

# CAROLINA MUSTARD SAUCE

## MAKES ABOUT 375 ML (13 FL OZ/1½ CUPS)

Both North and South Carolina are all about the pork, which pairs so beautifully with mustard. This sauce is bright and tangy, with a hint of sweetness.

### INGREDIENTS

185 g (6½ oz/¾ cup) American (yellow) mustard
2 teaspoons Worcestershire sauce
1 tablespoon ketchup
90 g (3¼ oz/¼ cup) honey
80 ml (2½ fl oz/⅓ cup) apple cider vinegar
1 teaspoon celery salt
1 teaspoon black pepper
½ teaspoon garlic powder

### METHOD

Put all the ingredients in a bowl, stir to combine, then transfer to an airtight jar. Store in the fridge for up to 10 days.

# ALABAMA WHITE SAUCE

## MAKES ABOUT 375 ML (13 FL OZ/1½ CUPS)

Made famous by Big Bob Gibson Bar-B-Que in Decatur, Alabama, award-winning barbecue guru Chris Lilly carries on the tradition today. This is unlike any barbecue sauce you've had before, and is served almost exclusively with smoked chicken. Though the core ingredients are vinegar and mayo, most folks add in one or two signature extras to make it their own. This is mine.

### INGREDIENTS

230 g (8 oz/1 cup) mayonnaise
80 ml (2½ fl oz/⅓ cup) apple cider vinegar
60 ml (2 fl oz/¼ cup) apple juice
2 tablespoons lemon juice
1 teaspoon garlic powder
¼ teaspoon cayenne pepper
1 tablespoon prepared horseradish
1 teaspoon Creole or dijon mustard
kosher salt and freshly ground black pepper

### METHOD

Put all the ingredients (except the seasoning) in a bowl and whisk to blend. Add salt and pepper to taste, then place in the fridge for about 1 hour before using, to allow time for the flavours to mingle. Store in the fridge for up to 1 week.

# HOME-MADE HOT SAUCE

**MAKES ABOUT 375 ML (13 FL OZ/1½ CUPS) THICK SAUCE OR 250 ML (9 FL OZ/1 CUP) THIN SAUCE**

Making your own hot sauce is much easier than you may think, and the fiery liquid will keep for months in the fridge. You can experiment with different flavours and levels of heat by using different types of chillies. For a sauce with a little less sting, omit the chilli seeds.

## INGREDIENTS
225 g (8 oz) chillies, stems removed
1 garlic clove, peeled
3 teaspoons kosher salt
185 ml (6 fl oz/¾ cup) white vinegar

## METHOD
Put the chillies and garlic clove in a food processor and pulse a few times until combined, then stir in the salt.

Scrape the mash into a large sterilised jar and cover with muslin or cheesecloth (something to stop anything getting in, but allowing it to breathe). Leave at room temperature for 5–7 days, to give the flavours time to develop.

For a thick sauce, stir the vinegar into the chilli mash after fermentation and store in an airtight jar.

For a thinner, more traditional Louisiana-style sauce, pass the mash through a sieve, then add the vinegar to the remaining juice and transfer to a clean bottle. Store in the fridge for up to 6 months.

# BUFFALO DIPPING SAUCE

**MAKES ABOUT 500 ML (17 FL OZ/2 CUPS)**

All the tangy spice you love in a buffalo wing is given a creamy edge when served with this sauce—double dipping is going to be inevitable! I've paired this sauce with Pickle-brined chicken nuggets (page 48), and you should also try it with my crispy Beer-battered onion rings (page 176).

## INGREDIENTS
230 g (8 oz/1 cup) mayonnaise
250 g (9 oz/1 cup) sour cream
1 teaspoon onion powder
1 teaspoon dried chives
1 teaspoon garlic powder
1 teaspoon paprika
60 ml (2 fl oz/¼ cup) hot sauce (ready-made or see recipe, left)

## METHOD
Put all the ingredients in a bowl and stir to blend well. Store in an airtight container in the fridge for up to 1 week.

# JALAPEÑO 'CRACK' SAUCE

## MAKES ABOUT 220 ML (8 FL OZ)

I nicknamed this sauce 'crack' because I'm completely addicted to it. I use it on tacos, smoked meats, grilled chicken, eggs and even as a dipping sauce for tortilla chips.

### INGREDIENTS
4 jalapeño chillies
¼ onion, peeled
1–2 garlic cloves, peeled
125 ml (4 fl oz/½ cup) vegetable oil
2 teaspoons lime juice
1 teaspoon kosher salt

### METHOD
Put a small saucepan of water on the stovetop and bring to the boil. Put the jalapeños and onion in the water and simmer over low heat for 10-15 minutes until softened.

Drain the water and remove the chillies and onion. Remove the seeds and stems from the chillies, then place the chillies and onion into a high-sided container for blending. Add the garlic cloves, vegetable oil, lime juice and salt.

Using an immersion or stick blender, blend all the ingredients together for 4-6 minutes, until well emulsified. Store in the fridge for up to 2 weeks.

### SWAP IT OUT
You can substitute the jalapeños in this recipe for any other kind of fresh chilli. That way, you can experiment with different flavours and spice levels. Try fiery habaneros for a fluorescent orange finish, or a milder poblano for a more delicate heat.

# STOCKS

Home-made stocks are essential in any kitchen. Not only do they add a wonderful depth of flavour to your cooking, but they are often much lower in salt than store-bought versions. Once made, stocks can be portioned and frozen as needed, and can be used for many of the recipes in this book. There are lots of variables that can affect the final volume of stocks, so yields will vary. You should expect to get roughly 8-10 cups of stock per recipe.

## OMI'S CHICKEN STOCK

### MAKES ABOUT 2 LITRES (70 FL OZ/8 CUPS)

My grandmother, or Omi, serves this 'stock' as her signature chicken soup every Friday night. It's her rustic version of a consommé, loaded with noodles or boiled potatoes. I always have containers of it on hand in my freezer.

### INGREDIENTS

1 kg (about 2 lb) raw chicken frames/carcasses, plus giblets
6–8 chicken wings
1 celeriac
2 parsnips
2 large carrots
3 celery stalks
1 brown onion, skin on
3 garlic cloves, peeled

### METHOD

Put the chicken frames, giblets and wings in a large stockpot. Roughly chop the celeriac, parsnips, carrots and celery into three to five pieces, and add to the pot. Cut the onion in half and add to the pot, along with the garlic cloves.

Pour in enough cold water to cover the veggies and bones. Slowly bring to the boil over medium heat, then reduce the heat to low and simmer gently for 3-4 hours. Scrape and discard the 'scum' that bubbles to the surface every so often.

Strain the soup into a large pot and discard the bones and veggies, then refrigerate overnight. Remove the fat that collects on the surface and the stock is ready to use.

# SLOW-COOKER BEEF STOCK

## MAKES ABOUT 2 LITRES (70 FL OZ/8 CUPS)

Beef stocks require many hours of slow cooking to extract flavour and build body. I never liked the idea of leaving a stove on overnight (for safety reasons), so I came up with this version, which uses a slow cooker to handle the 24-hour cook time.

### INGREDIENTS

1.5 kg (about 3 lb) mixed beef bones, including oxtails
2 tablespoons olive oil
2 carrots
2 celery stalks
1 brown onion, skin on
4–6 button mushrooms
2 garlic cloves, peeled
1 tablespoon whole peppercorns
2 tablespoons apple cider vinegar
1 small bunch flat-leaf (Italian) parsley
2 bay leaves

### METHOD

Preheat the oven to 200°C (400°F). Line a large baking tray with foil.

Coat the beef bones in olive oil and arrange on the tray, then transfer to the oven and roast for about 45 minutes. The bones should brown, but do not let them burn.

Cut the carrots and celery into two to three pieces, and quarter the onion. Put them in the slow cooker, along with the whole mushrooms, garlic cloves, peppercorns, vinegar, parsley and bay leaves. Add the browned bones and then pour in enough cold water to cover the bones, plus an extra 4 cm (1½ inches) of water on top.

Turn the cooker on low, cover and cook for at least 12 hours, and up to 24 hours, occasionally skimming off any scum that rises to the surface. Strain the stock and cool, then refrigerate or portion and freeze. For a clearer stock, strain the stock twice using muslin (cheesecloth) for the second pass.

# RUBS, SEASONINGS AND GLAZES

Rubs and seasonings will keep for months at a time in the pantry; just make sure to store them in an airtight container, out of direct sunlight. Glazes are applied towards the end of cooking, to give a glossy and sweet finishing note.

## PICKLING SPICE

### MAKES ABOUT 50 G (1¾ OZ)

This is the spice I use for curing pastrami (page 123), but it's also a great all-purpose mix for pickled veggies, too.

**INGREDIENTS**

1 cinnamon stick
4 bay leaves
1 tablespoon black peppercorns
1 tablespoon brown or yellow mustard seeds
2 tablespoons allspice berries
2 teaspoons caraway seeds
8 cloves
2 tablespoons coriander seeds
2 teaspoons ground ginger

**METHOD**

Break up the cinnamon stick into smaller pieces, and crush the bay leaves to break them up. Put the cinnamon and bay leaves in a bowl, add the remaining ingredients and stir to combine. Store in an airtight jar. This spice mix will keep for months.

## BASIC BRISKET RUB

### MAKES ABOUT 345 G (12 OZ)

The key to a successful brisket bark has a lot to do with the size of the pepper chunks. Pepper is usually measured in size by 'mesh', and the ideal size for beef rub is anywhere between 10 and 16 mesh. It's a very coarse crack, sometimes referred to as crushed or kibbled.

**INGREDIENTS**

215 g (7½ oz/1½ cups) black pepper
130 g (4½ oz/½ cup) kosher salt
50 g (1¾ oz/¼ cup) garlic powder (optional)

**METHOD**

Combine all the ingredients, adding the garlic powder if desired, and store in an airtight container for up to 1 month. It will keep for longer, but the pepper will begin to lose potency over time.

BASIC BRISKET RUB / PAGE 206

**PORK SEASON-ALL DRY RUB / PAGE 209**

# CAJUN SEASONING

## MAKES ABOUT 150 G (5½ OZ)

Cajun seasoning is used in place of regular salt in many kitchens across Southern Louisiana. It's the staple flavour of my Cajun brick yardbird (page 61) and a key ingredient of Rice and gravy (page 153).

### INGREDIENTS
2 tablespoons kosher salt
2 tablespoons cayenne pepper
2 tablespoons paprika
2 tablespoons garlic granules
1 tablespoon freshly ground black pepper
1 tablespoon onion powder
1 tablespoon dried oregano
2 teaspoons white pepper
1 teaspoon dried thyme

### METHOD
Put all the ingredients in a jar, firmly screw on the lid and shake to combine. The seasoning will keep for months at a time, though the pepper and some other spices start to lose their freshness and brightness over time.

# PORK SEASON-ALL DRY RUB

## MAKES ABOUT 230 G (8 OZ)

Ribs, chops or butts, this paprika-laden dry rub is a best friend to pork. Apply liberally, particularly for low and slow cooks.

### INGREDIENTS
110 g (3¾ oz/½ cup, firmly packed) light brown sugar
30 g (1 oz/¼ cup) sweet paprika (not smoked or hot)
2 tablespoons kosher salt
1 tablespoon chilli powder
1 tablespoon onion powder
1 tablespoon garlic powder
1 tablespoon freshly ground black pepper
1 tablespoon mustard powder
2 teaspoons ground cumin
1 teaspoon cayenne pepper

### METHOD
Combine all the ingredients and store in an airtight container for up to 6 months.

# SWEET RIB GLAZE

## MAKES ABOUT 375 ML (13 FL OZ/ 1½ CUPS)

You can't get sweet, sticky ribs without a great sweet, sticky rib glaze. The jam and reduced apple juice are a perfect complement to pork. Slather up to three coats of this glaze liberally across your ribs towards the end of cooking.

## INGREDIENTS

750 ml (26 fl oz/3 cups) apple juice
250 g (9 oz/1 cup) ketchup
125 ml (4 fl oz/½ cup) apple cider vinegar
125 ml (4 fl oz/½ cup) water
1 tablespoon Worcestershire sauce
2 tablespoons strawberry or plum jam (without any fruit pieces)
2 tablespoons light brown sugar
2 tablespoons sugar
1 teaspoon garlic powder
1 teaspoon onion powder
2 teaspoons paprika
½ teaspoon cayenne pepper
½ teaspoon freshly ground black pepper
2 teaspoons kosher salt

## METHOD

Pour the apple juice into a saucepan and simmer over low heat until the mixture has reduced by at least half and has the consistency of maple syrup.

Put all the remaining ingredients in a second saucepan over low heat and stir to combine. Stir in the apple syrup and gently cook for a further 20-25 minutes. Allow to cool, then store in an airtight jar in the fridge for up to 2 weeks.

## COOKING TIP

Remember, this super-sweet glaze has been designed for low and slow cooking where the temperatures do not get high enough to burn the sugar. If you plan to use it for grilling, it may be best applied right at the end of the cook to avoid any unpleasant charred tastes. You can also experiment with different jam flavours, such as apricot or cherry.

# FINISHING SALTS

Finishing salts are flavoured salts that can be used as a final-addition sprinkle to boost the taste of a completed dish. Of course, you can always use them as regular seasonings at any stage of the cooking process.

## SICHUAN PEPPER SALT

### MAKES ABOUT 90 G (3¼ OZ)

Use this salt on seafood, pork and spicy fried chicken.

### INGREDIENTS
4 tablespoons kosher salt or sea salt flakes
2 tablespoons sichuan peppercorns

### METHOD
Combine the salt and peppercorns in a small frying pan and toast over low heat for 5–8 minutes until fragrant. Be cautious not to let the peppercorns burn. Allow to cool, then transfer to a spice grinder or mortar and blend or crush until powdered. Store in an airtight container.

## PORCINI SALT

### MAKES ABOUT 75 G (2½ OZ)

Sprinkle this earthy salt on pasta, steak or add it to gravy. You can adjust the ratio of salt to mushroom depending on your preferred taste.

### INGREDIENTS
10 g (¼ oz) dried porcini mushrooms
65 g (2¼ oz/¼ cup) kosher salt or sea salt flakes

### METHOD
Put the dried mushrooms in a spice grinder or coffee grinder and pulse until they become a coarse powder. Add the salt and pulse until the mix is a fine powder. You may need to work in batches to avoid overcrowding the grinder. Alternatively, grind the mushrooms and salt using a mortar and pestle.

Store in an airtight container and sprinkle on your favourite foods for a serious umami kick.

# SMOKED ROSEMARY SALT

## MAKES ABOUT 270 G (9½ OZ)

Use this smoked salt on lamb, fries or roast beef. The larger porous sea salt flakes do a better job of absorbing the smoke faster than other salts, so it's the preferred kind for this recipe. Finely ground rosemary (or rosemary powder) can be found in specialist food stores and delis. If unavailable, use dried rosemary leaves and grind them into a fine powder using a spice grinder or mortar and pestle.

### INGREDIENTS

3–4 rosemary sprigs
2–3 wood chunks
2 cups wood chips (preferably a strong-scented wood such as hickory)
260 g (9¼ oz/2 cups) sea salt flakes
2–3 teaspoons finely ground dried rosemary

### METHOD

Put the rosemary sprigs in a bowl of water and set aside to soak for 1 hour, then drain. Prepare a charcoal grill for two-zone cooking. Throw the wood chunks and chips onto the coals and allow the smoke to start forming and the grill to heat—this should take 2–4 minutes.

Pour the salt into a baking pan or aluminium foil tray and spread out evenly across the base. Place the pan on the indirect side of the grill, then add the rosemary sprigs to the coals. Close the lid and cook for at least 45 minutes, or until the smoke subsides. Cool the salt, then toss with the ground rosemary. Store in an airtight jar.

# CABERNET SALT

## MAKES ABOUT 250 G (9 OZ/1 CUP)

Use this salt on roasts, lamb and even desserts. I prefer to use fleur de sel for this recipe, as it has a more pronounced grain that seems to soak up the wine a little better and has a chunkier finished appearance, but you can use kosher salt or sea salt flakes if you wish.

### INGREDIENTS

500 ml (17 fl oz/2 cups) cabernet sauvignon
200–300 g (7–10 oz/1–1½ cups) fleur de sel salt

### METHOD

Pour the wine into a saucepan and place over medium heat. Cook the wine until you are left with only 2–3 tablespoons of liquid, making sure it doesn't burn as it becomes more syrupy.

Turn off the heat and slowly stir in 1 cup of salt. If there is excess wine, add the remaining half cup. The salt will appear very damp, like wet sand.

Line a baking pan with baking paper. Spread the salt in the pan and set aside to dry (this can take up to 1 day). If you have a dehydrator, use it to speed up the process. Store your vividly red wine salt in an airtight jar.

CABERNET SALT / PAGE 213

SMOKED ROSEMARY SALT / PAGE 213

PORCINI SALT / PAGE 212

SICHUAN PEPPER SALT / PAGE 212

# INDEX

# THE MANY NECESSARY THANK YOUS

This book came to fruition with the support of many awesome people. First, a huge thank you to Peter Bouchier, Butchers of Distinction, in Melbourne, Australia, for providing all the meat for the recipe photos. To USA Foods, who helped me source all my crucial American ingredients for the shoot. To the publishing team: Jill Dupleix, Jane Morrow, Emma Hutchinson, Hugh Ford and Kim Rowney. To Lee Blaylock and Mark Roper for your droolworthy visual abilities. To Anthony and the Southern Boys Barbecue team for letting me hijack your smoker. Continued thanks to Aaron, Kristina, Isabel, Demelsa, Brother Billy, Noomsy, Jay, Adam, ABA crew, PK Grills, Pitts & Spitts and many more who should be named, but know I am grateful.

Published in 2017 by Murdoch Books, an imprint of Allen & Unwin
Reprinted 2018, 2019

Murdoch Books Australia
83 Alexander Street
Crows Nest NSW 2065
Phone: +61 (0) 2 8425 0100
Fax: +61 (0) 2 9906 2218
murdochbooks.com.au
info@murdochbooks.com.au

Murdoch Books UK
Ormond House
26-27 Boswell Street
London WC1N 3JZ
Phone: +44 (0) 20 8785 5995
murdochbooks.co.uk
info@murdochbooks.co.uk

For Corporate Orders & Custom Publishing, contact our Business Development Team at
salesenquiries@murdochbooks.com.au.

Publishing Consultants: Jill Dupleix and Terry Durack
Publisher: Jane Morrow
Editorial Manager: Emma Hutchinson
Designer: Hugh Ford
Project Editor: Kim Rowney
Photographer: Mark Roper
Stylist: Lee Blaylock
Production Manager: Lou Playfair

A cataloguing-in-publication entry is available from the catalogue of the National
Library of Australia at nla.gov.au.

ISBN 978 1 76052 257 5 Australia
ISBN 978 1 76052 760 0 UK

A catalogue record for this book is available from the British Library.

Colour reproduction by Splitting Image Colour Studio Pty Ltd, Clayton, Victoria
Printed by Hang Tai Printing Company Limited, China

IMPORTANT: Those who might be at risk from the effects of salmonella poisoning
(the elderly, pregnant women, young children and those suffering from immune deficiency
diseases) should consult their doctor with any concerns about eating raw eggs.

OVEN GUIDE: You may find cooking times vary depending on the oven you are using.
For fan-forced ovens, as a general rule, set the oven temperature to 20°C (70°F) lower
than indicated in the recipe.

MEASURES GUIDE: We have used 20 ml (4 teaspoon) tablespoon measures. If you are
using a 15 ml (3 teaspoon) tablespoon add an extra teaspoon of the ingredient for each
tablespoon specified.